Endorsement by the book reviewer

When one achieves some success in life, the sense of accomplishment is exhibited through joy. As humans we are programmed to repress joy. That is because we leave unopened most of what is required for us to experience joy. In 1 Kings 2:3, King David tells his son Solomon to do what the Lord commands and follow his teachings. Notice that David is not asking his son to build his kingdom by gathering wealth for himself or to assemble great armies to win battles; rather the joy of success here lies in following and obeying God.

In our society today, joy is the state of great delight or happiness. Success on the other hand is the sense of achievement that we feel when we accomplish something.

Most of us withhold exhibiting any kind of joy until we accomplish a specific goal, at which point we pull it out. We frequently exhibit joy on weekends, during thanksgivings and on holidays. It is little wonder why we run out of steam very quickly. Much of what we need may simply be a little playfulness, curiosity, passion, awareness, creativity, wonder, intuition, optimism and some level of imagination. These are what children possess that enable them to experience much joy and are the very things that highly successful people possess that help them accomplish extraordinary results.

This book "The Joy of Success" by Tochukwu Okafor has a lot of insights. Enjoy the Book.

Well done Tochukwu.

Paul Emeka, PhD

"Based on observations and experience, success is measured by those micro and macro accomplishments that fulfill one's life on a daily basis—it is also a psychological and social construct that has its presence on how one views life. In other words, if an individual who decides in the morning to be optimistic even in the face of challenges, and accomplishes such goal at the end of the day can claim to be successful. Therefore, success is subjective to one's view about life—as it is a daily journey that can bring joy to an individual who is intentional to self."

J. Ibeh Agbanyim, author of *The Power of Engagement: How to Find Balance in Work and Life*

THE JOY
of
SUCCESS

WHAT IT MEANS TO TRANSFORM SUCCESS INTO EXCELLENCE

TOCHUKWU OSITA OKAFOR, MPA

iUniverse, Inc.
Bloomington

THE JOY OF SUCCESS
WHAT IT MEANS TO TRANSFORM SUCCESS INTO EXCELLENCE

iUniverse books may be ordered through booksellers or by contacting:

iUniverse
1663 Liberty Drive
Bloomington, IN 47403
www.iuniverse.com
1-800-Authors (1-800-288-4677)

ISBN: 978-1-4759-8399-9 (sc)
ISBN: 978-1-4759-8400-2 (hc)
ISBN: 978-1-4759-8401-9 (e)

Library of Congress Control Number: 2013905874

Printed in the United States of America

iUniverse rev. date: 4/5/2013

Table of Contents

Foreword

I met Tochukwu Okafor when he first started working for Arizona Department of Corrections (ADC) back in 2006. I was his supervisor, and he impressed me with his honesty and integrity. When I first saw this gentleman, I saw a star in the making. When he approached me with the honor to write the foreword for his book, it was not a surprise to me that such an ambition would come from him. This book, *The Joy of Success*, really sums up the attitudes he has about the importance of hard work, education, and personal responsibility. These things, plus his faith in God, and his own personality, are what make him a successful man. He knows that we do not all start out successful, but what is important is how we finish, and what we did to get there.

Everyone has his own idea of what success is, but to Okafor, it means using your talent, education, life experience, and other positive means to do what he calls "transform success into excellence." By this he is talking about making positive changes in the lives of others who may not be as fortunate as you are, those who may need a positive influence in their lives, and so making your community better as a result.

Besides telling you what you need to do to be successful to this level, he also warns you about things you should try to avoid because they will get in the way of achieving the success you want.

The first thing you have to do before you can be a successful person is to decide what you think your purpose in life should be. You need to make a list of dreams and try to achieve at least one major item each year toward making this list a reality. As you work on this, you need to forget about any failures or shortcomings that are in your past. Do not let anyone tell you "no" or "you cannot," and remember that most successful people are not smarter than you are. Whatever background you came from, do not use it as an excuse not to be successful. Before you can begin to achieve the joy of success, though, you need to find out what your talents are.

Okafor defines talent as, "The natural skill or gift given to every individual that has extra ordinary control over destiny." Once a person discovers what his talent is and begins to work in that area, everything in his life will start to fall into place and success will result. If you are not sure what your talent is, what can you do? Okafor suggests trying as many things as you can to find out what you are good at. After that, you can use it and make yourself known for whatever it is. He uses some wonderful examples of professionals and athletes as well as his life to express the fact that success is a continuous occurrence.

Tochukwu Okafor still works for ADC, but today he has a Master's degree in Public Administration and is directing public policy programs. He worked very hard to earn this degree and was encouraged along the way by his supportive family. He found out what he is good at and became successful at it, which gives him great satisfaction and joy, and that will lead to excellence as he gives back to his community and to the world. As he says, "Success embellished with excellence is equal to ultimate power."

The Joy of success is exciting. I am sure that all who read this book will not be disappointed.....Enjoy and good luck with your new success!

Kevin A. Ziebell
State of Arizona

Preface

The Joy of Success was prompted by series of thoughts. I have asked myself why some people are happy, and some are not. Some people are rich, and some are poor. Some people are successful while some are not. I figured that people should know that success is a vital phenomenon in human existence. I stand as a living testimony to the fact that one's life is continually evolving. You should not let yours be stagnant because "without continual growth and progress, such words as improvement, achievement, and success have no meaning" (Benjamin Franklin). That is why the world is but a rolling stone. What you have called a comfort zone should be your starting point. I see no reason anyone should settle for less because with **vision** and **ambition** the road to success is bright.

There are a few examples of transformation of life in the book that should inspire you to aspire higher. The book teaches the meaning of success and the joy of experiencing success. It kind of amazes me what it means to transform success into excellence. You will see the elucidation of that phrase in the introductory part of the book as well as in subsequent chapters. What matters in life is not how you started, but how you ended. In other words, the end justifies the means.

The book gives you the proper understanding of the whole concept of success, which comprises of emotional stability, financial breakthrough, attainment of goals, happiness in marriage, job satisfaction, discovering of talents, prosperity, and so on. It discusses in detail excellence that cannot be achieved without success. Therefore, your success is not complete until it reaches excellence. It thereby has not reached excellence if you positively have not impacted the community or the society as a whole. Inasmuch as the book emphasizes much on education as one of the keys to success, it also covers a vivid explanation of the things you **can do** if you have the desire to achieve success. The lucid intention of *The Joy of Success* is to bring to the audience a message of **hope** and **enlightenment**. What makes it different from other books is the fact that it empowers you to **greatness**.

Do you have a dream? Most successful people have dreams. Therefore, do not let your own die just like that. Success is not just having a dream, but the practicality of reaching the point of self-actualization. Success is not just having a job, but having job satisfaction. Success is not starting school, but graduating from school. Success is not living in America, but being productive in America. Success is not just getting married, but staying married. Marriage is the most difficult institution on earth. It is indeed more difficult than college. So since we all have our weak points, it is necessary to look into the things that can improve our marriages. Enjoy the book and wait for your success. *For your information, the actual names of **most** characters in this book are withheld for privacy purposes, but the examples used are all true life stories.*

Introduction

Definition of success depends on one's perspective. What you call success may differ from what I call success. According to Webster Dictionary, success is 1. The favorable or prosperous termination of attempts or endeavors. 2. The attainment of wealth, position, honors, or the like. In my opinion, the positive end product of an adventure or a plan is success. Someone who had an event, and there was no fight, accident, or any form of disappointment would say it was a success. Also, someone who started school and eventually got graduated, notwithstanding the storms of every academic program has achieved success. In success, there is prosperity, and in prosperity, there is **joy**.

Having made a tremendous effort to be in the United States of America for the sole purpose of achieving success, I have come to realize that academic excellence is not only very important, it is a powerful tool in attaining success. Therefore, it is everyone's obligation to study hard and get the best grades that will prepare them for the challenges of today's workforce and business opportunities. I have to agree to the notion that success is next to excellence, and if I achieve success then I seek excellence. It has been evidently proven that Michael Griffin, a physicist and aerospace engineer who was the chief administrator of NASA until 2009 and was also named by *Times* in 2007 as one of their 100 most influential people did not achieve such success being indolent; rather through incessant educational commitments.

I was born to a father, Chief J. U. Okafor who believed strongly in education and was a principal supervisor of schools by profession. When I was growing up, I admired him so much because of his high degree of integrity and unquestionable reputation. He was a role model to many people because he challenged his personal impediments with excellence. His pursuit of excellence led him through so many rigorous hurdles of trials and tribulations. His fame could not have materialized by just his natural intelligence, but the knowledge acquired through higher learning. Knowledge is power and half education is dangerous. Being a son of an educationist, I strongly believe that my success will come after I have attained a high level of education and not to dwell on past glory.

An English Poet, William Wordsworth commented about man's obsessive concern with material things that have no lasting benefits. As a scholar, I hereby state that I will rather invest my money in education, which eventually will give me business ideas, technical know-how, and overall success in life than to be in this challenging world of today and fail to appreciate the **voice of education.**

In my understanding, the word "excellence" means perfection. It is therefore indeed a quality that gives strong demarcation between superiority and inferiority. Who wants to be inferior in the world of today? I am certainly not the one. What I am saying in essence is that excellence that comes through success makes one famous, different, and outstanding. Excellence gives one confidence and paves ways for 'ultimate power' regardless of race, color, or/and natural origin. Excellence is your first class ticket to greatness. "Be not afraid of greatness: some are born great, some achieve greatness, and some have greatness thrust upon them" (William Shakespeare). I had an event that was full of glory. As I was thanking one of my friends, Mike for their support in making me look great. He replied, "Tochukwu you are naturally a great man." There is absolutely nothing wrong in claiming greatness because whether you like it or not, it must surely manifest if it is meant to be.

Top grade point average (GPA) can earn someone a scholarship. It can land someone a very lucrative job where people will have no choice but to know you regardless of your parental background. The president of the United States, Barack Obama for example, has been opportune to sit on the highest and most prestigious seat in the world because his academic excellence has brought him an ultimate success. At this time, no one cares if his father was from Kenya in East Africa or if his mother was abused by his father. Here, success has overshadowed hindrances.

My interpretation of success is not just money or wealth, but going to the best schools, studying the right courses, and keeping the highest GPA. My high school principal, Timothy Anigbogu would say and I quote, "Seek you first academic excellence and every other thing will be added unto you." You should be optimistic so that your relentless efforts in your schoolwork and other endeavors of life will see you through as you look forward to the success ahead. "Faith without works is dead" (James 2:20). A Christian brother, Engineer Jason has excelled beyond people's comprehension at his Intel job because of his intellectual inclination and personal demeanor. Despite his impressive achievements, he is still humble and has never for one day taken God's glory. Here we are speaking of one who lives a life that is worthy of emulation.

However, when good education is attained, every other thing will be gradually put in place. It is called success. Wealth or money will come, but when you become successful, poor people should benefit from your financial assistance. What about impacting positive social change in the lives of less privileged people in the communities and across the globe? What about running a nonprofit organization that could change the world? What about those ideas to become an entrepreneur? Success does not stop at being smart or graduating from college. It actually begins from there. It is never complete until you are able to **transform success into excellence**. You may be wondering how that happens. It is done by making use of your certificate, knowledge, money, and even experience to change the lives of others. Educate people to know what you know. Show younger generations the keys to success. Share with church members and others around you what you did to succeed. Try to give others the chance to get employment at your workplace. If you are a supervisor, consider empowering your subordinates. Help one another because you do not know where your help will come from when you are in need. Despise nobody and despise not the days of small beginnings.

Again, my idea of success is not sitting and receiving benefits from the federal, state, or local government; rather, it is working hard to transform your story into greatness. In other words, it is more blessed to give than to receive. Success will be completely called excellence when you can use your wealth of knowledge to help the sick people in their various homes. Success should be able to save lives and deliver people from danger. When I am able to build schools, hospitals, and good roads in some remote parts of Africa, my success will be said to be excellent.

Most importantly, trained teachers will be empowered and attracted with sufficient salaries. In some parts of the world, teachers are neglected or rather under estimated and thereby are underpaid. Someone who has reached the level of excellence can single handedly use some political powers and change that perception. I will conclude this phase by reiterating that to have success is to seek excellence and to have excellence is to have what it takes to impact positive social change in the lives of less privileged, and the society as a whole.

Chapter 1
Finding your purpose in life

There is a reason you were created the first place. There is a reason you find yourself where you are at the moment. There is also a reason you are a medical doctor or a teacher. That reason is your purpose in life. If you have never asked yourself a question as in what your purpose in life is, the time to do so has come. Locate a conducive place where there is absolute tranquility, sit comfortably there, and meditate over your purpose in life.

Successful people are usually individuals with sense of purpose. They are strong willed human beings with **vision** and **ambition**. They will rather try and fail than not to try at all. According to Ella Wheeler Wilcox, there is no fate, destiny, or power, which can hinder, control, or circumvent the firm resolve of a determined soul. Do you have the determination to succeed? Do you have a sense of purpose? What have you sacrificed for success? Finding your purpose in life is essential, and when you do so, other things will fall into place. Life will start making sense.

A person with a sense of purpose is never idle. He or

she is always looking for ways to invent new products. He is always looking into any opportunity to become an employer of labor. He dreams big and takes risks. A person with sense of purpose does not relax and become comfortable with just paychecks. Whoever that relies on paychecks alone goes from paycheck to paycheck. Just paychecks will not make you a millionaire. If you have the determination to succeed, you should make friends who reason alike. Stay away from friends who will be pulling you down whenever you are climbing the ladder of success. Avoid the company of the pessimists if you desire success.

Most times people find it very difficult to change environment, change business or career. It is quite understandable, but you can never go wrong stepping forward. Your purpose for example might be to move to Iraq so you can bring peace to the land. The point is that things might be rough, but as soon as you obediently make that move of faith and relocate to Iraq, things will change for good. Take a look at what happened to Jonah when he was told to go to Nineveh and preach the gospel of God. He did not want to do it. In an attempt to run away from God's sight, he got caught up with nemesis. Eventually, he did it but after going through much adversaries just for disobedience.

The boldest step I have taken in my life is not coming to America, but leaving my comfort zone in Newark, New Jersey, to come to Arizona of all places. On that faithful morning, I put my eight month pregnant wife, Linda in the car as well as my 18 month baby girl, Uche headed to Arizona. I drove 2512.58 miles from New Jersey to Arizona to complete a journey of four days. This draws us back to my definition of success---*the positive end product of an adventure or a plan.* The journey was a great adventure. The trip was a success because my wife did not give birth to my second child in the car and in the middle of nowhere, but a month later. Circumstances could have triggered labor while on the road, but the grace of God that surpasses the determination of faith saw me through.

If you want to find your purpose in life, write down on a piece of paper what you have done in the past, what you are doing now, and what you want to do in the future. The most important of all is *what you really want to do in the future.* Even though your past experiences can help you develop your future and bring your purpose to a fulfillment, it is also recommended to make a wish list. Write down everything you wish to accomplish for the year. Paste them on your mirrors, on your office desk, and in your bathroom. Each time you look at them, tell yourself that you must not give up until you have them accomplished. Do not let any year pass you by without at least one major accomplishment.

If you want to build a house, for example, do not wait until you become a millionaire. Of course, you will be a millionaire, but you have to keep striving until then. When you are talking about building projects, it is always a big expenditure, but do not let that scare you away from your purpose. Some people have the money in bulk but some do not. Therefore, if you do not, putting money bit by bit will gradually but definitely get you going and will eventually finish it. It also depends on how determined you are. Your determination in completing a house might require cutting down on clothes and other unnecessary expenses. It is then the time to apply the basic economic concepts of scale of preference and opportunity cost. You just do the very necessary things for the mean-time. The rest can wait; after all, they are not imminent.

When you are working and have never thought of putting

some portion of your income away for the rainy days, you need to think twice. There is going to be a time when you cannot work anymore. There is nothing wrong in investing money in stock, real estate, mutual funds, 401K, life insurance, and so on. Even putting away $200 every month will give you $48,000 after 20 years of your hard labor. If you take $48,000 and retire in a country with low cost of living, you will be okay. This amount of money will not make you to be considered rich, but will help you get started with another phase of life. Success is all about planning.

What about those citizens on the street of Flatbush in Brooklyn, New York, who have sworn not to ever keep a job. There is no success in indolence. They wake up in the morning, put on their white summer t-shirts and just hang out in front of the high-rise apartment buildings all day long. It definitely will take a miracle for you to make it staying idle. Taking government benefits is good but can never make you rich. Do you have a dream, or you just want to eat and sleep? Do you live to eat or you eat to live? You are supposed to eat to live because if you live to eat that means your concern is just to live and eat. I am not a philosopher but I believe the logic is not too much of a critical thinking for us.

Our younger generations in junior high and high schools need to step up their games. The time is past when you say, *"I do not wanna go to college."* Make it compulsory that you will go to college come what may. You have to define a future for yourself. Your parents just need to give you their supports, but the determination to be educated is yours. When you are graduated from high school at the age of eighteen, no one at this time can push you against your will. That is why I encourage you to see the importance of education. An educated person for the most part will live above poverty level at least. Do not put retardation to your growth.

There are so many bad things to avoid if you go to school. They say that an idle man is a devil's workshop. When you are not keeping your brain busy with academics it will start thinking about crimes. The eight hours spent at school is more meaningful than eight hours spent on the Internet (facebook and chat rooms). Internet is a good servant and also a bad servant in the sense that it can ruin you. Some Internet sites are not safe for the children. Do not get me wrong, information technology has made it possible even for us to sit home and research extensively online without going far for it, but always consider its disadvantages to our idle children. Unhealthy relationships are developed there online. Make good use of your time and build a relationship that will yield profit. **Girls, stay as tight as you can.** High school pregnancy most times ruins your chances to progress. It is only on very rare occasions that you come back to make it after giving birth while still in high school.

Challenge yourself and advance beyond your own imagination. Do not look back when you are focusing on the future. Do not let your friends bring a stumbling block in your desire to become an icon of success. Success is not meant for one particular race or ethnicity, but anyone with a sense of purpose. If you have a sense of purpose, there is no way you will agree to spend your entire life in incarceration. Even if you have been a victim of bad choices, get up and move on.

Say no to poverty

Poverty is defined in Webster Dictionary as:
1. The state or condition of having little or no money, goods, or means of support.
2. Deficiency of necessary or desirable ingredients.

If you have never experienced poverty, you will not understand how bad it is to be poor. A poor person does not dream of buying a car because he cannot even afford a tire. He does not dream of buying a house because he cannot afford a studio apartment. Most poor people cannot boast of eating three times daily because they have no means of steady income. There are limited resources for a poor person. Nobody chooses to be poor, but some people have refused to challenge the spirit of poverty. Some rich people today were not born rich; they simply say no to poverty.

Oprah Winfrey was not born rich, but she strove hard to overcome hardship. She was actually born in rural Mississippi to a teenage single mother. Oprah had been ranked the richest African American of the 20th century. She was not given more chances than other Americans. She just was able to focus on her priorities. If your priority is to dwell on the past, you will not have the zeal to focus on the present or the future.

It is true I have emphasized much on education. I know some people will be wondering about those multimillionaires who did not go to college. Well that is where destiny comes in. If your destiny is poverty and you decide to challenge it with education, you will end up being average (middle-class citizen). Meanwhile, if your destiny is poverty, and you accepted it and remained adamant about it, you will definitely stay poor. Education just gives you an edge over the ability to grab wealth when the opportunity comes. "A higher education gives a person an edge financially, emotionally, socially, as well as intellectually. It is something you will always have that can never be taken away, no matter what you ultimately choose to do with your life" (Ron Credio, Warden).

Implications of poverty

1. Poverty can cause death
2. Poverty can cause sickness
3. Poverty can cause lack
4. Poverty can cause accident
5. Poverty can cause divorce
6. Poverty can cause depression
7. Poverty is a disease.

Here are some points to ponder

- Vision and ambition lead you to success
- Finding your purpose in life helps you to stay focused
- You have no excuse not to achieve success because it is not meant for certain category of individuals
- Whatever you do, get education because it is one of the strongest tools to success
- Abstain from immorality if you have desire for success
- Let go of distractions (it could be friends)
- Avoid the company of the pessimists if you have the desire to move forward.

Chapter 2
The enormous magic in positivity

It is true people always want to believe that someone is against them. Having always kept at least one job in any given time here in the United States, I have discovered that workers worry more about their colleagues or supervisors than anything else. Employees always think that someone is out to get them fired. In fact, there is too much pressure working here in the United States, especially in the nursing profession. There is always one witch standing and looking over their shoulders in search of fault. These people go to work in **fears** and come home in **tears**. They face uncertainties each moment they are out to their various workplaces. I have met one who would tell me "Yeah they do not like me because I am this and that." Do you know that it is good to stay **positive** while being focused? It is actually better not to worry about those things even when you knew that they exist. Worries will never solve your problems; rather they will compound them. "Too many of us are not living our dreams because we are living our fears" (Les Brown). Everyone is not going to like you, but you have to challenge yourself hard enough to get to the point where even your accent will not deprive you of your position or blessing.

However, if your coworkers or supervisors like you, you definitely will last in a job. They contribute so immensely to your wellbeing (happiness). They affect your level of productivity. Therefore, since we all know that for sure a co-worker or a supervisor can make one's life miserable, the best approach is to remain **positive** and listen to that voice of education. Do not escalate a situation that might require just a dialogue. Believe in yourself and do not get easily intimidated. Rebuke anxiety and tension because they can make you look stupid, meanwhile; you are not.

When was the last time you said to yourself "**yes I can**?" Of course you are capable of surmounting the situation that is giving you sleepless nights. How about praying and believing that it is well? Shakespeare said that a coward dies many times before his death. Here is an instance. Angela Grace was a family friend who was told by a medical doctor that her left leg would need to be amputated because of a complication of ulcer and diabetes. She became so afraid and worried. She passed away even before the scheduled date of surgery just because of fear. According to Psychology Today, **fear** is a vital response to physical and emotional danger, if we did not feel it; we could not protect ourselves from legitimate threats. But often we fear situations that are far from life or death, and thus hang back for no good reason.

The more positive you are about life, the more successful you become as a person. Workplace discrimination will never end, but why should you be the victim of circumstances? Stay positive and try to add a little more substance to your attributes. The fact is that there should be something extra ordinary in you that should actually make you better than others, or rather something that makes you unique. It could be dressing. What about education? You do not have to be the smartest person to get educated, but once you get it, you are automatically different. By all means, you need to stand out. That is the only way you are recognized. If your employer or boss sees that you have nothing to offer, he or she will tend not to waste resources on you, because *"time is money."*

There is a coworker who recently obtained his Master's degree. When others were taking promotional examination, he refused to participate. His reason for refusal was because he believed that people would laugh at him if he failed the examination. Why do you want to put a limitation to your potential? "We need to steer clear of this poverty ambition, where people want to drive fancy cars and wear nice clothes and live in nice apartments but do not want to work hard to accomplish these things. Everyone should try to realize their full potential" (Barack Obama). Try to positively be a believer for once and see the ***enormous magic in positivity.***

Someone who knows me too well right from my youth days in New Jersey once stated, "Tochukwu is successful because he is likeable." I hereby charge you today to make yourself likeable, and you will experience success. Gossip does not make one successful. Not letting go of the past does not make one successful, either. It makes you bitter whenever you set your eyes on the person you believed that offended you 10 years ago. You can be successful in such a way that when you are ever in need of something that thing will just come to you without you reaching for it. Gabriel Okoye stated, "When I was a youth, I never lacked anything. As I grew up, events started changing. Here comes suffering, tension, anxiety, and frustration. It is this time that I realized that the world is but a stage. Full of contradictions of life."

Come on now! It is all about your attitude. One with positive attitude must believe that the latter days should be better. It is quite okay not to lack anything as a youth, but when you grew up, it is time to make other people around you not to lack anything. Do not see responsibility as suffering; rather, see it as a push to success. I am not writing this book as a lamentation toward your 'pity party' but to inspire you to have a high aspiration. Lament no more and possess your possession. Even if it takes violence, just do it. After all, "The kingdom of heaven suffereth violence and the violent take it by force" (Matt. 11:12). However, when you already knew that your heart is a temple of God, and you went ahead and locked someone in there, you have automatically locked in your success.

Reject Negativity

As we have seen the need to stay positive, let us go down to the reasons to reject negativity that can pose as a hindrance to our successes. I came in contact with someone who entered my office speaking with such a weird voice. When I asked him why he was speaking like that, he said, "It is because I have Multiple Personality Disorder [MPD]." I came home that day and asked my wife, Linda, who is a registered nurse if there is anything as MPD, and she said yes, "There is a case as Multiple Personality Disorder." Why is it so easy for us to admit that we have one thing or another? You have to reject it by all means because it is not your portion. It is only in this country that I have heard of too many unfamiliar diseases and disorders.

On a different occasion, I met a mother (Crystal) who was really worried about her first child who was diagnosed with Selective Mutism. Selective Mutism is a social anxiety disorder characterized by not speaking to specific people or in specific venues. It is a specific variation of obsessive compulsive disorder. Crystal and her husband were called to meet with the school officials to discuss a possible way of helping their child. The only possible option they had for the parents was to recommend putting the child on medication, only because she was always too shy to speak in the class. As a matter of fact, she would never say a word to anyone while at school. The mother of the child who has never been an advocate of medication said, "No way, my child will not be put on any medication. I reject that in Jesus Name." Today, the child is probably the best student in her class. She is not afraid anymore to communicate with teachers, students or even strangers. Challenge your obstacle with positivity. Reject bad thought and negative speech. Do not claim sickness or failure. A successful man is he who does not succumb to the evil wish of the devil.

Metamorphosis of Life

The metamorphosis of life starts when a baby is born. The stages he or she goes through as in growth and development is what I call metamorphosis. As a human being is going through growth and development, he or she engages in life changes. There is a time to play with toys. Here comes a time to start school. It gets to a point where one says, "When I grow up I will like to be a doctor." Now you start having dreams. But if just having a dream is enough to make one achieve success, well there should not be any reason teaching about the keys to success. Having a dream is good, but it is primary. Just as my child, Uche had once said, "I wish all dreams could come true." Dreams will come through when you put the dreams to work. *The practical application of keys to success is the pillar behind every successful individual.* Where have you left your desire to achieve success?

Life itself is metamorphosis. Richard was born and raised in a remote part of the world (in a third world country) where basic life necessities were regarded as luxury. In other words, Richard did not experience the joy of electricity and running water growing up. He finished elementary school before he saw television for the first time. Today, he is in the United States with abundant luxury commodities to enjoy life with, even though his wife still calls him a village champion (VC). Richard today has been able to provide his village people with free pipe borne water. This is one of the things he lacked growing up. Success has made it possible for him to help the community. God bless America.

I have investigated extensively from successful people and have discovered that **honesty** and **integrity** are also strong tools in achieving success. You have to build a good reputation if you want to progress in your business. Honesty they say is the best policy. When your business dealings are as transparent as they could be, you are heading to winning the hearts of your customers. When you win the hearts of customers, you achieve success. The success of a business is continuity and turnover. If your company cannot back up its products with honesty and transparency, you start losing customers. When you start losing customers, chances of making it will be very slim, but when you stand by what you say and portray positive image of the company you represent, you will be successful.

My business trips to different parts of the world have exposed me to the fact that many traders out there will cheat (trick) you in a heartbeat if you are not paying attention. The thing is that when you are cheated, you are not going back there. They will not own your business anymore. So which one is better? Eating big today and have nothing tomorrow or eating bit by bit in a continuous manner?

Discovery of talent combined with positive attitude will produce success. Bitterness of heart combined with vindictiveness will produce depression. The outcome of laziness and carelessness is sloppiness. Pessimism and sadness will result to poverty. Meanwhile, joy and success will produce excellence. Finally, success embellished with excellence is equal to ultimate power.

Here are some points to ponder

- Be hopeful as you focus on your goals
- Worry not about who wants you fired because it can only increase your anxiety
- Avoid living in fear because fear is an enemy of progress
- Apply honesty and integrity in your business so you can achieve positive results
- Having a dream is good but will not make you achieve success unless you put it to work.

Chapter 3
Discover your talent

Talent is a natural skill or gift given to every individual that has extra ordinary control over destiny. A man's gift makes a way for him. The reason it is very important for everyone to discover his or her talent is because the moment you do so, life will start making sense. It is basically where your destiny lies. Sometimes, a talented child is discovered at a very tender stage, but too many of us beat about the bush for a long time before we are able to discover our talents. Some people may have to try many courses at school to be able to find out the ones they are good at. The appalling part of this whole thing is not being able to discover your talent at all. I think it is better for this discovery to be delayed than to be denied entirely.

I could remember my high school classmate, Kenneth who was brilliant at the time. One day he told us, "When I grow up, I will go to Japan and I will be one of the engineers making fans." He knew exactly what he wanted to be and he said it to us. He was not guessing and was not putting probability in his statement. He was quite assertive. Today,

Kenneth is an electrical engineer; he has traveled to Japan for some special trainings and experience, and he is currently working for Shell Oil Company.

Joseph was a dreamer. He also had the talent of interpreting dreams. He never for one day took his talent for granted. He kept interpreting dreams even when his brothers were jealous of him. When he was sold into slavery by his jealous brothers, his gift made a way for him. His master had a weird dream and needed an answer or the meaning of that dream. Joseph who was nobody was summoned to interpret the dream. He did the job so perfectly without any fear or favor. He then got promoted and became the most powerful man in Egypt next to Pharaoh. He became a God sent who later saved his family members from famine. His brothers and even father later bowed down for him so that his dream would come to a fulfillment...*A dream come true.* This whole dream would not have manifested had it been Joseph failed to overcome the trial of sleeping with his master's wife as she instigated. But despite all, he was still able to forgive his brothers who wanted him dead by all means. How humble can you be when your dream comes true? How forgiven can you be when you become successful?

If you want God to help you succeed in life, you need to first of all discover your talent. When you do so and channel your effort toward that, success follows. Otherwise, you will see yourself taking the longest route to your destination. What do you have in you that can be used to bless you? Are you an eloquent speaker? Are you a good singer (with wonderful voice)? You have to sit up and consider using your voice to make money. Your voice is a gift and not a right. If you do not use it, you lose it. When you are blessed with a golden voice and instead of using it to praise God or release music album; you are busy cursing and condemning everyone that comes around you. Some people are indeed using their talents for the wrong reasons.

There is a governor with so much money who uses his money on prostitutes. His priorities are mixed up. His talent is wasted on wrong choices. One thing is to discover your talent. Another thing is to use it efficiently and effectively.

I happen to be fortunate enough to meet one man whose voice I admire. Whenever he sings, I am moved. He discovered his talent. He joined the choir and later became a pastor. He is currently using his voice to serve the Lord. His voice alone is capable of drawing sinners closer to God. Eyes cannot see what his voice has done in many people's lives. Some people will rather have him sing along with the choir every time... **the power of talent**. Ignore not the gift of God.

Emmanuel is an African soccer player who started playing on the street of Ajegunle, Lagos. He got discovered by an agent. The agent worked hard and got him connected to one of the English Premier League clubs in England. Today, he has successfully flourished. His talent made him a very successful youngster. His life transformed from street player to a highly rated professional player. What a good way to show off what you have got in you.

Dikembe Mutombo is another African immigrant (from Zaire, The Republic of Congo) who came to the United States to study medicine. When he was participating in the University's basketball practice, the coach (John Thompson) discovered the talent in him. He called him aside and had a conversation with him. He basically told him that he had displayed some extra ordinary skills in basketball. He emphasized that he should consider a career in the game. He listened to the advice and followed his destiny that has been discovered. Low and behold, he turned out to be one of the most successful basketball players in the United States. Today, he has Dikembe Mutombo Foundation that is focused on health, education and quality of life for the people of The Republic of Congo. Dikembe Mutombo has had numerous accomplishments, which include but not limited to the following: In July of 1999, he shipped medical and pharmaceutical supplies to Kinshasha. In November of the same year, his foundation shipped 140 hospital beds to Congo. It was also recorded that in September of 2000, he shipped the only working ambulance to Kinshasha as well as computers.

He has had the opportunity of having personal dealings with many prominent personalities like former president of the United States, Bill Clinton; Microsoft guru, Bill Gates; South African Anglican Archbishop, Desmond Tutu; former United Nations Secretary-General, Kofi Annan to mention but a few. The over seven foot tall African immigrant is an epitome of excellence. He has excelled in academics, sports, and humanitarian activities. He became one of the best shot blockers in NBA. This led to his achievement of winning NBA Defensive Player of the Year Award for four times. It is a record breaking (highest) statistic in history of NBA. Dikembe Mutombo is ever grateful to John Thompson. How many times have you forgotten the people who God used to change your life? **How many times have you condemned the person who moved you from your Egypt to a Promised Land?** How many times have you bit the finger that fed you? If you want to achieve success, appreciate the good deed of man first.

Hamilton is a close family friend who got an admission to study Mathematics at University of Nigeria, Nsukka. He had wanted to study Mechanical Engineering. After his first semester, he got switched over to Mechanical Engineering at his request. It did not take more than a year for him to realize that he did not like Mechanical Engineering as a major. Bear in mind that this young man was highly intelligent. He started looking for a way to change to a more challenging major because he thought that Mechanical Engineering was not as challenging a major as he expected. Obviously, Hamilton was unable to discover his talent despite his high degree of intelligence. Just out of frustration, he ended up dropping out of the university. The climax of Hamilton's story is that in 2001, when I traveled to Holland, I saw him loading 40 foot containers for traders. So his inability to discover his talent made him deviate from being an engineer to becoming a truck loader. Do not you ever miss your time and chance. Moreover, we all need to remember that you do not have to be in certain professions to be successful. Just discovering your talent while focusing on priorities can make you achieve success.

I cannot emphasize any further on the importance of knowing your skills. Try many things and figure out which of them you are good at. There is going to be at least one thing you know how to do. If you have found out what you can do, do it and do it right. Specialize in it and make yourself a wanted commodity. When it is you and no other duplicate of you, you are automatically indispensable. If you leave a company, they will miss you. If you put out your resume, companies will be running helter-skelter in your pursuit. Make yourself important.

By all means, if you cannot speak well, try to write well. Either of the skills can pave your ways into success in school, in business, and in your social life. Kenny G. is an American adult contemporary and smooth jazz saxophonist who did not have a breakthrough success until after his fourth album, Duotones in 1986. What am I trying to prove here? Because you have a talent does not mean that your very first venture will be a success. No! You can still try multiple times before you succeed. Also one attempt can uplift you beyond measures, but you have to stay focused.

One thing is picking the courage to try something first. The next is being patient when things do not go your way the very first attempt. Do not be in a hurry to judge yourself. Do not conclude by saying, "I am not good." You are good, but you just do not realize it. You have got the ability to excel in what you are doing. Therefore, do not let anyone tell you otherwise.

I am sure someone out there is asking questions about the lives of some celebrities. Yes, so many high profile talented celebrities ranging from Mindy McGready to Michael Jackson have ended so prematurely. It has nothing to do with their ability to discover their talents. It's just that fame goes two ways. When you are famous, it is your choice to live a decent life or a reckless life. It is absolutely recommended to live a good life when your time comes, because as you make your bed, so you will lie on it.

Here are some points to ponder

- Do not misuse your talent on wrong choices
- Do not be in a haste to achieve success; sometimes good things do not come so easily
- Appreciate the people who helped you discover your talent

- Find out what you have in you that can be used to bless you
- Do not operate below your potential
- When you achieve success, do not stop there; seek excellence
- Do not ever look down on yourself.

Chapter 4
Be your own motivator

Most times people look for someone to motivate them. It is okay to look up to someone and it is okay to listen and acquire knowledge, motivation or inspiration from someone. It is good for you to also realize that the truth you told yourself is better than the truth someone else would tell you. In other words, "Always bear in mind that your own resolution to succeed is more important than any other" (Abraham Lincoln). Nothing gives you more confidence than believing in yourself. The worst thing that can happen to you as a human being is looking down on yourself. When you have never trusted yourself that you can do anything big, how do you want other people to believe in you? When the opportunity to move forward is right in your hand, but lack of self-confidence will not let you step up, it is indeed a big problem.

It has come to the point when people need to start making right choices and stop blaming parents, friends or enemies. We all have fallen short of expectations in one way or another, but we cannot let our past hold us down forever. Eighty five percent of inmates we work with at Arizona Department of

Corrections (ADC) believe that it was someone else's fault that they are incarcerated. One of them even said that his father had never advised him to go to school; that his father taught him how to steal. I would rather let go of the past and make necessary adjustment that can overshadow my past mistakes. Your father has his life to live, and you have yours to live. Your decision to achieve success in life is solely yours and for your own dignity. "The difference between a successful person and others is not a lack of strength, not a lack of knowledge, but rather a lack of will" (Vince Lombardi). Develop a strong will and believe that if success is in any way attainable that you can achieve it.

When you are out there counting what people have not done for you, how many times have you counted within yourself what you have done for others? Many of us are also always checking what God has not done for us without appreciating the things He has done for us. When every failure of your life is always another person's fault, why do not you for once pause and find out what you are doing wrong? When 99.9% of people you have had encounter with offended you in one way or another, maybe it is time to ask yourself a question. Maybe furnishing answers to these rational questions can bring positive results in the future.

I still believe that 'downfall of a man is not the end of his life' as they always say. That is why you should not be afraid to fall but should be ready to get back up and make the most out of life. As a young lonely man in New Jersey, I never looked back in my strong desire for success. I tried many things and failed many times, but **I did not quit trying**. I will not hesitate to disclose that in my first year in the United States, I got admission for my first degree at William Peterson University in Wayne, New Jersey, but lack of a reliable car, inadequate financial support, added with tough classes contributed to my failure to succeed. "Failure defeats losers, failure inspires winners" (Robert Kiyosaki). I dropped out of college and waited until fall of 2000 to go back to a different college. In fall of 2004, I came out of New Jersey City University (NJCU) with a Bachelor of Science degree. The truth is that school was hard and to make it worse, I had to do two jobs as a full-time traditional student. There were bills to pay, too many parking tickets and traffic violations to settle, and too many people to take care of back home in Africa. Did all of these make me despondent? No, because my personal philosophy has always been that despondency is the worst melancholy. I was not a genius, but a little bit of luck and abundant grace of God saw me through my undergraduate wrangle. My eight years in New Jersey were full of interesting experiences that actually helped to mold me into who I am today.

I had a precious opportunity to interview an education supervisor of Arizona Department of Corrections (ADC) Eyman Complex, George Arhin. When I asked him what he understands by the word "success." He replied that success does not have an ending point. In other words, it is a continuous process. We both had a constructive debate on the word **success**. I found out that we actually arrived at the same point by using some examples as: If someone succeeds in getting Associate degree, he wants Bachelor's degree. When he is done obtaining Bachelor's degree, he desires for Master's degree etc. So in Mr. Arhin's opinion, success is endless accomplishments. I enjoyed that kind of positive thinking and wished there was enough time to continue that conversation.

If you accomplish one thing and think there is no point striving for higher, you definitely have no vision. Anyone with lack of vision sees no growth. On a different occasion, a mentor, Dr. Paul Emeka made me to understand that success can make you to actually grow out of your job, but you have to motivate yourself for higher accomplishments.

It has come to my realization that one should always endeavor to help, especially when you can afford to, regardless of the outcomes. A general opinion of the public identified some problems in rendering help to people. Six out of ten persons helped would turn out being offended or expect more than what you the helper can offer. The point is that there is no way you can please everyone. It is therefore recommended to do what you can do as human and let destiny take care of the rest. When the person you have helped is somewhere cursing you or smearing your name, God is somewhere blessing you the more.

Instead of waiting for someone to come and push you into doing something big for yourself, why do not you do those big things and people will be motivated by you? Prove to people around you that you are not a *"nobody"* as they all regard you. Show some extra ordinary qualities so you can scale through the hurdle of being looked down upon. Life experience has so far taught me to always try to prove them wrong; I mean those who see you as a slow or incompetent person...prove them wrong. I prove them wrong by passing the exams they cannot pass. I prove them wrong by coming out top three in an examination. The law of equality knows no slow person. Success does not discriminate against the below average students in your class, neither does it discriminate against people of different cultural background at your work place. Therefore, do not operate below your capability. Show the world that you possess a strong will to succeed.

When I first came to the United States from Nigeria at the

age of 23, I could have gone back home for good and avoided the whole suffering of being alone in a foreign land with no relatives and under bizarre weather condition of New Jersey, but I chose to motivate myself. What matters is not how I lived in Newark Liberty International Airport for two days or how I lived in someone's car for two weeks, but where I live now. What matters is not what my family went through in the process of letting me travel abroad, but how much of joy, life, and hope have I brought them in return? What matters is not how I slept on the floor without mattress in a very cold New Jersey weather condition, but where I sleep now. Leave those who complain about this land of opportunity (America) because they know no better. They need to consider relocating elsewhere so they will understand life better and maybe value what they take for granted. Just make use of your time because it is an essential commodity.

Building anticipation toward a set goal gives you the excitement to look forward to its attainment. Set your goals and prepare on starting to work on them. Map out the strategies to follow and look forward to getting into it. That is what I mean by building anticipation. You motivate yourself by remembering the implications of failure. When you know how disastrous it is to fail, that awareness will push you through striving for success. In a situation you did not succeed, remember not to give up because **perseverance** is the key to success. I have noticed that whenever I have a plan and I did not disclose it to anyone, there is always a tendency of not carrying out that plan; after all nobody knows. On the contrary, whenever I have a plan and I make it known to someone, I will definitely accomplish the plan, because I hold myself accountable for every word of my mouth. Find out the techniques that work for you and use them as you focus on your vision and ambition.

Many people do not believe that dressing good matters. According to Traphagen, few are unaware of the value of clothes that make them look more attractive, more prosperous, and successful. Sometimes we forget to realize that for the most part, we are judged by the way we are dressed. A woman has no reason not to look attractive. Looking attractive at the same time does not mean looking naked. When you look naked as a woman, you have defeated the whole purpose. Good things attract excellent things. Good dressing attracts good suitors.

When you are going to a job interview, you have no reason to look shabby. They say by their fruits we shall know them. If you are carelessly dressed, your potential employer would think you are going to do a careless job. How decent you look tells how good of a job you are going to do. Indeed, first impression matters. Your physical appearance that shows perfect grooming has a long way to go in your desire to be selected for a job. There is a proverb that says that you will eat a child's face before eating what he has. Someone's deportment and speech are essential, but the best of all is the attraction of first look. It works like a magnet. You cannot go wrong with this. "Dress does not make the man, but it often makes the successful man" (Disraeli). Do not let your opportunity to be selected for a high position be dismissed due to your inability to dress well and appropriately. Dress clean because cleanliness is next to godliness. Even though it is not always true that carelessly dressed individuals do rough works, but the truth is that good dressing increases your chances of achieving success.

The Black Sheep Syndrome

When you are regarded as the black sheep in your family, you will be treated with so much hatred. People will look down on you. You will have no value before your peers. Sometimes, you will feel isolated. You feel like changing, but you cannot. You will be seen as one who will never achieve anything in life, but the reality of life is that once a black sheep is **not** always a black sheep. If you have been called names or despised upon, I know it affects you psychologically but the spirit in you can turn things around for you and for good.

People do have too many reasons to fail but do not let those reasons hunt you down. I grew up knowing Chavez. He was always missing school. In fact, he was the most stubborn boy I had ever seen. Whenever he left home for school, he would end up getting into trouble in someone's house. One day Chavez was caught stealing someone's bike. He nearly got killed because people usually beat thieves to the point of death. Some matured men in the community pleaded on his behalf. So he was given another chance. He looked back and realized that he had been causing his parents so much pain and had brought disgrace to himself and his family. He cried unto God and repented. Today, Chavez is a medical doctor. A black sheep has become a medical practitioner. Do we all deserve a second chance? I will leave the question for you to answer.

Some people are called names because they have been doing things that brought such name calling. Also, some people are called names just out of mere hatred...for no just cause. Either way, none of them pleases the person you are referring to or God. Words of our mouth are very strong and can go a long way unless there is a divine intervention.

Divine intervention is a supernatural rescue from above. You are judged by what comes out of your mouth. Your tongue can save, and it can destroy too. Some people are in serious dismay today because of what came out of their mouths. I have seen someone who used his mouth to swear against his own health.

I have learned from church teachings that the success of your children starts from what you the parents prophesy/confess upon them. For example, if you keep calling your children idiots, they will grow as idiots. Idiots do not have common senses. So when your children are grown with no common sense, you should blame nobody but your tongue. Say unto a child what you wish for him or her. Charity begins at home. Therefore, the foundation of success is laid by parents. Discipline your child when he or she misbehaves, but do not curse him or her. If you as a parent lay good foundation on your child, that child will never forget you. Success is not just having children but raising them with fear of God. When they have the fear of God which is the beginning of wisdom, they will do the right things that will lead them to achieving success.

Here are some points to ponder

- Motivate yourself and go beyond your own imagination
- One of the characteristics of success is multitasking
- Challenge your obstacles with positive results
- Control the words of your mouth, and confess positively regardless of your situation
- Avoid calling people names because it does not please the person involved or His creator.

- You might have failed many times in your attempt to achieve success, just know that the end justifies the means
- First impression matters in everything we do
- Train up a child in the way he should go for when he grows, he will not depart from it.

Chapter 5
In the middle of life
struggles, be yourself

It is quite understandable that life itself is full of ups and downs. Many of us have even voiced it out that life is not fair. I'm not writing this to prove or to claim that life is fair, but to make you understand that in any circumstances you find yourself, try to be yourself. Do not lose your value as human and do not lose your personality as a professional.

As a child, it might look like a bed of roses, but when you grow up you find out that it is survival of the fittest. I have noticed that weaker minds tend to give up so easily. You have no reason to give up on yourself when you are faced with the difficulties of life. Never you use the phrase, "I cannot take it anymore." When everything seems to be going wrong, what you need is nothing but patience for a patient dog eats the fattest bone. Even though some predicaments are more precarious than others, but many people have been through the exact same predicament you are in today. So, do not think that it is you against the world.

In the mist of tribulations, if you are married, cling onto

your spouse. If there is lack of harmony between a couple, when external squabbles (or any form of attack) come, the magnitude of the blow that is going to hit them can detach the union. But when you fight an external battle with oneness, you are guaranteed a winner.

How many times have we asked ourselves why people do what they do? Why do some people smoke and some do not? Why do some people drink and some do not? Why do some people drive high-end cars and some insist on driving their cheap old cars? The reality is that everyone wants good things but not everyone can afford them. Men are created equal, but all fingers are not. When you cannot afford high-end cars, be yourself and do not engage in fraudulent activities so as to belong. It is called competition and can lead to sin or crime, but if you are succeeding and someone else says that you are competing, ignore it and keep moving. "Always be yourself, express yourself, have faith in yourself, do not go out and look for a successful personality and duplicate it" (Bruce Lee).

Everyone is not destined to be a multimillionaire, but everyone is given equal chance to succeed. After all, "It is not of him that willeth, nor of him that runneth, but of God that showeth mercy" (Romans 9:16). The gentle Portia in *The Merchant of Venice* by Shakespeare said that "Mercy is the fundamental aspect of human existence." If someone has shown you mercy in the past, what have you shown in return; appreciation or ingratitude? On the other hand, it is an overstatement or rather a stereotype to say that the world is full of ingratitude. **Everybody is not an ingrate, but many people tend to ignore the power of appreciation**.

As a college student, you are exposed to all kinds of lifestyles. If you have never had the desire to smoke, why would you allow peer pressure to lure you into the habit of smoking? It is true this makes you accepted as part of a group, but at this time you are not being yourself. The same thing is applicable to those groups of people who use drinking to compete. Be yourself and seek success. The people with those habits are actually struggling to quit, and you are somewhere trying to emulate them so as to belong.

Whatever you want to do in life, listen to your **voice of education** and ask God for guidance. Do not let friends or family members push you to the wall because the damage might be irreparable. When your father or mother is making a life partner choice for you, always remember to explain to them that you are the one directly involved and not them.

Staying married

If you value your marriage, you have to sacrifice in one way or another. Be you a man or a woman, but if you are a man, be a man and challenge your obstacles with determination. In every successful marriage, there is one peaceful person. I challenge you to stand as a symbol of peace in your family. It is your family anyway. Therefore, the peacefulness of your marriage lies on you.

If you are already married, I will not ask you if you are married to the right person because it is already too late. If I start asking that, it is what they call medicine after death, but if you are still looking, please look well and do it once and for all. There are too many things you cannot do if you have a broken marriage. If you aspire to become a politician, divorce can hunt you. A popular figure needs to be upright with no strings attached. A good leader is expected to lead by examples. The followers or subordinates should be able to look up to you. As a matter of fact, if you are destined to be the president of your country but due to some unforeseen circumstances, you find yourself divorced, it has automatically ruined your chances. Do not be a destiny killer against your own destiny.

It is perceived a wrongdoing to write or teach about marriage, success or prosperity if you have a dysfunctional home. It is true that money for the most part is the source of major marital issues people have in the Western World, but by all means try to work it out. It has long been generalized that women do not know how to talk, but recent incidents have proven that even men speak louder, more vulgar, and even more annoying than some women. You should learn how to cool your temper before speaking to your wife. If your wife is being the talkative, remain silent, and leave the area. "Silence is golden" and two wrongs cannot make a right.

The key to the door of success is given to the man of the house, but behind every successful man there is a woman. You cannot go wrong by believing in the truth. If you are a man, use wisdom to control every situation in the house. In general, the politically correct notion is that men are more intelligent than women. You are expected as a man to apply your intelligence always without making your wife feel inferior or belittled doing so. Though, these days women do not admit anymore being the weaker vessels because almost everything men do in this twenty first century, women do them too, if not better. The only way you can make this clear to them is by handling situations right and using your brain to multitask. When you intervene in a critical and difficult situation, the way you handle it says it all. You do not need to fight over who is smarter, because action speaks louder than voice. Show what you got and **keep your marriage** going. **Staying married** is the most prestigious gift for anyone who desires success. I call "staying married" a gift because bad things can happen to anybody---*It is only by the grace of God that many of us are staying married.* I am not an angel, neither is my spouse and devil does not like the word marriage from the word go. That is why he usually comes with the entire army of soldiers to steal, kill, and to destroy marriages.

On the other hand, if your marriage has failed due to one reason or another, you still need to stay as positive as you can. It is not the end of the world. Perhaps, you have tried your possible best not to go that route (divorce), but you just could not help it; well thank God that you are alive, and move on with your life. Rationally, I understand that there are some situations that are beyond your control as human, especially when a marriage is full of torture and abuse. It is not healthy for both parties, and it is only the grace of God that can turn things around in that case.

Most importantly, say no to polygamy. Polygamy (where they practice it) has never turned out good. It is bloody and deadly. There are always cases of fighting for rights, love, and for properties. It is a disaster and should be discouraged by all means. For those of you who do not know; it is traditionally acceptable to have more than one wife in Africa. That is exactly what I call polygamy. The reason for that, I cannot tell you, but I just know that it brings all kinds of quarrels. When a woman is sharing her husband with five other wives, she might one day start imagining how great it would feel to be the most loved one. First of all, how can you be the most loved when there was no love there to start with? It is practically impossible to love six wives at the same time. Some people are being fooled.

Reasons for crimes

In my survey of why people commit crimes, majority of the offenders said that they commit crimes because they had never thought about being caught. Just imagine this, one would wake up and decide to go rob a bank and make so much money without rationally weighing the consequences. That is absolutely true. If you think twice before you do what you do, there is possibility of realizing that the outcome might be unfavorable to you. Nemesis must always activate the winds of fate. There are consequences for every wicked deed of men.

This whole ideology of being yourself goes into what I call *the execution of **critical thinking***. First of all, my very own definition of critical thinking is a way of reasoning right, acting with caution, and weighing options rationally before executing a plan. On the other hand, it is defined by Paul and Elder (2006) as "The art of analyzing and evaluating thinking with a view to improving it."

The use of critical thinking and my understanding of it have given me the ability to make good judgments pertaining to whether to continue my graduate program or to suspend it. At a point, the program became too hectic and stressful, especially when considering my full-time job, business, and raising three children. It was time to apply critical thinking. Then I gathered and assessed relevant information as well as consequences of eventually dropping out of the program. Also my excellent grades so far in the program left me with no choice but to continue striving for success. For the fact that a critical thinker "communicates effectively with others in figuring out solutions to complex problems" (Paul, Elder, 2006), it became easier for me to share my worries with my wife, Linda and was able to accumulate substantial reasons to persevere. Tony Robbins stated that you should identify your problems but give your power and energy to solutions. Critical thinking helps you to minimize mistakes. It enables you to make informed decisions as well as sound judgment. The problem-solving ability is very important in every management, research, and practice; because it assures good results for efficiency.

Life is a process

There is absolutely no shortcut in life. You have to pay your dues if you want to achieve success. Some people want it big and fast, but having shadowed successful people so closely, I have come to a conclusion that life is a 'step by step process.' Life itself needs application of spontaneous overflow of wisdom. If wisdom is not applied, there might be regrets in the future. The very few individuals who reject the application of wisdom in their self-interest desire to make wealth end up serving time.

If you open multiple computer applications at the same time just because you are so much in a hurry, you will end up slowing the computer down. The computer has to communicate with the other processing applications and report to the CPU, which is the Central Processing Unit. In the process, it is either it causes delay or it shuts you down and tell you that the program is not responding because an error has occurred. Now which one is better? Taking it step by step but slowly, or crashing the system in the name of fastness? Fast lane has its bad side because what goes around comes around. There is a reason why you have to attend Elementary School before High School. You count one before you count two. If you attempt to skip, you have obstructed a free flow process of life. If you are looking for a shorter way (short-cut) to your destination, it might take you even longer time to discover it. Just go with the flow.

Success takes patience. When you have sown the seed of success, you have to patiently wait for the right time to enjoy the fruit of your labor. Will you rather take small bite of cake and have it every day for your consumption or finish your cake in one day and starve for the rest of your life. It is an easy methodology. You cannot eat your cake and still have it. In other words, you cannot burn your bridges and expect a miracle. I so much believe in miracle, but we should also face the reality of life.

Here are some points to ponder

- Know what you want and stick with it
- Do not let friends and family push you to the wall
- Do not let people make choices for you; do it and take responsibility
- Take control of your future, but with God
- Be patient in choosing your life partner because a stitch in time saves nine
- Follow the step by step process of life and accomplish your goals
- There is no love in polygamy
- Remember to always apply critical thinking in your life endeavors
- Try your best to save your marriage, but if it involves physical abuse (assault), seek professional advice. Do not lose your life.

Chapter 6
Education for responsibility and its impact on public sector

Education molds one into a responsible being. God created you and means well for you, but how do you help yourself? You help yourself by taking advantage of the opportunities available for you. Education is one of the opportunities. In all you do, get educated. Education is fundamental to America's societal and economic future; however, many people take it for granted. "You really need to excel far above if you want to be considered for anything in this country" (Oluyinka Olutoye). The education you get will not only help your personality but will also impact the nation positively through your expertise.

Therefore, it should be a requirement in every household to get educated; it shouldn't be an option. According to Houston Chronicle, the survey conducted by Rice University shows that **Nigerian immigrants have the highest levels of education here in the United States**. Nigeria makes up a very tiny portion of the U. S. population, but believe it or not, 17% of them held Master's degrees while four percent had

Doctorate degrees. American Community Survey conducted in 2006 by the U. S. Census Bureau confirmed that 37% Nigeria Americans had Bachelor's degrees. In comparison, eight percent of the white population in the U. S. had Master's degree. One percent held Doctorates. About 19% of white residents had Bachelor's degrees. Asians come closer to the Nigerians with 12% holding Master's degrees and three percent held Doctorates (Census survey).

Advance technology for higher learning has paved ways for computer and civil engineers as well as medical professionals. In today's health care industry, there are state-of-the-art computerized machines used in saving lives. The use of computer to monitor the heartbeat of patients is high-tech and requires skills. Computer-controlled imaging devices such as computerized axial tomography (CAT) scanners and magnetic resonance imaging (MRI) are important tools for diagnosis. Computer-controlled surgery is far more accurate than the surgeon's unaided hand. Those computers and even MRI machines are definitely not going to operate themselves. The nurses, doctors, and technicians make use of them. How can you be responsible for those lives being put in your care if you did not get educated on how to use the machines?

An African mother (Ekwutosi) visited the United States and was not aware that she was diabetic. The very day her daughter in-law checked her blood sugar, she discovered that the woman had blood sugar of 588. She was taken to a doctor where she got immediate medical care. She was later educated on how to check her blood sugar and blood pressure. Now she is responsible for making sure that the readings of her own blood sugar as well as the blood pressure are at their normal rates...*education for responsibility.*

I have always heard that parents should educate their

children on safe sex. What about educating them that the best safe sex is abstinence? It is a win-win situation. Abstinence is the safest of all because you do not need to worry about so many other things that are involved. The more you know, the higher your chances to succeed. The power of education has no limit in reshaping our lives. It is the things you know that will save you; not the ones you do not know.

The knowledge of computer technology has made lives easier over the past decade. One important reason is the high quality application software (including word processing and spreadsheet software). These enable people to work at least part of their time at home, in closer contact with their families. Application software enables people to work efficiently with documents created in almost any line of work, including invoices, letters, reports, proposals, presentations, customer lists, newsletters, tables, and flyers. Word processing programs make writing easier.

Computers are playing an important role in the bid to make airline manufacturers create safer, more efficient designs, train better pilots, ensure safety in the air, and guide aircraft to safe landings. They are making airports safer and more convenient in dozens of ways. Smartcard-based access systems keep unauthorized personnel out of secured areas. Wind shear detection system warns pilots of dangerous downdrafts. Computer technology is so prevalent now that knowing how to use it is fundamental to being a member of modern society. It is by the means of this technology that millions of individuals gain access to the global connection system known as Internet. Internet is therefore the life wire of every business today. Knowledge enhances success. According to Academic of American Colleges and Universities, education involves more than the mind. It also involves developing students' personal qualities, including a strong sense of responsibility to self and others.

As a Public Administrator, there are some insights I want to unveil as we look into public sector. The United States public sector is basically the government. The government of the United States is therefore a very broad sector that comprises of the federal, state, and the local government. As the population of people is increasing, the impact of the United States public sector is increasing too as to be able to meet the economic demands of the United States citizens and residents. In other words, the government is doing so great in providing security services in our parks and public libraries; keeping the highways safe and clean for the public, and even providing all sorts of assistance to families in need.

Ever since the rapid growth of the United States population and the industrialization, there was an imminent need for the government to be stricter in laws and regulations. Immigration processes got tougher. Obtaining driver's license became harder to get in the sense that too many things are required. More people started immigrating to the urban cities in search of jobs, easy transportations, and pursuit of happiness. At this juncture, government has to put things in place so as to measure up with the changes. More public workers were employed. Effective public transportation systems were introduced with the use of trains and buses.

Despite the fact that the government provides the amenities for the public, there are still some criticisms that the government is taking control of everything, including invading people's privacy. It is only an ignorant that will not notice that the government has great impact on the public and the standard of living. The government has made the people of America to have sense of **responsibility**. It mandates one to pay his or her taxes when necessary. It makes people to be accountable for their actions in the sense that anyone who commits a crime does the time. Anyone who drinks and drives faces the consequences of a drunk driver.

Setting the speed limits for the motorists has saved lives and will always do, even though some people would argue that it is not fair to restrict people on how to live their lives. Setting an age limit on the sale of alcohol is a good influence by the government because it takes maturity to act maturely. In general, the impact of the government on the lives of American people and the economy has so far proven to be of tremendous positive social change in the quality of lives of Americans. "Thus, the subject matter of public sector economics falls into the two general categories of revenue generation and government spending" (Holcombe, 2006, p. 28).

For the fact that United States government has been budgeting and living in deficit, the decisions of expenditures are now based on the scale of preference. In other words, they spend money according to the order of priorities/importance.

The government allocates resources to the most appropriate places. Policymakers are involved in deciding where and what to put money into. Policymakers are believed to make informed decisions, and they do. This decision making is not made by one person but rather a group of intellects. Lawyers and policymakers collaborate, coordinate, and cooperate well to make informed decisions. They also try to check the positive and negative aspect of every situation before making decisions. A decision to prepare a balanced budget means making a budget to be at either equilibrium or surplus.

Here are some points to ponder

- Get educated in anything you do
- Education opens your eyes to responsibility and accountability
- Know your computers because you need the skills in a challenging world of today
- Most jobs now require computer literacy
- Equip yourself with knowledge and aim higher
- Abide by the laws so you can stay away from troubles
- Educate your children on the importance of abstinence.

Chapter 7
Beware of the three Ws

When I was about to travel to the United States, one of the most crucial advices my father gave me was to beware of the three Ws. They are **wine, women**, and **weed**. He said that for a man to be successful, he must abstain from the aforementioned three 'W' words. I said to myself, "What kind of advice is this?" I personally did not understand how a young and handsome man in his early 20s could avoid drinking or dating women. It looked impossible but I did not express my huge disagreement. It was not until I got to the United States that I realized that my father was right.

Wine, women, and weed will drain your pocket to the last penny. These three things will destabilize your focus. They can put you in jail. They are capable of ruining your life. When your mates are going to school so as to achieve success, your mind is preoccupied with these things that have no economic value whatsoever. There is no extra room in your brain to accommodate these obstacles. I call them obstacles because they are capable of standing in your way and deprive you the opportunity to move forward, but it is all about one's choices. When people are focusing on trading, schooling, or manufacturing; you find yourself revolving around the three Ws because they do not have parallel compatibility...*Beware of the three Ws.*

Wine

A football player recently got charged of intoxication manslaughter, a second degree felony because he had a drunk driving accident that claimed the life of his close friend and a teammate. He is under the custody of law enforcement officers awaiting his due process of law in the Criminal Justice System. Even though he has sent a message of regrets to the family of the victim, but it does not change the fact that drunk driving has done its worst once again. The talent of the offender is now doomed for life. What are your choices in life? When you are intoxicated, the senses become dulled, the vision becomes hazy, and the equilibrium is made unstable. This is when to do it all (I mean all the atrocities you can think of). A high percentage of convicted felons believe they did it because they were drunk. A young female adult who drinks her worries away in a bar has every tendency of waking up in a stranger's house the next morning. You know what that means. Drunkenness will make you do those things you will never imagine doing under normal circumstances.

Always ask yourself 'what am I known for?' It is recommended for one to leave a legacy. It should be something good that you will always be remembered of. Do not expect everyone to say well of you, but let majority do so. Follow your instinct and avoid the avoidable. If drinking is capable of putting you in lifetime probation and under some kind of monitoring device, then it is not worth it.

Women

Women are special creatures with special qualities. They were created to help the men. They are also capable of taking you straight down to your grave. Be wise so that you look well before you leap. If womanizing can make you lose your life to AIDS, what good is it? If womanizing can make you lose your family or rather your marriage which took a while to build, I do not think it will make you proud. Stay away from what does not belong to you because all that glitters is not gold. Do not waste your money and time unnecessarily for the sake of five minute enjoyment. Any time wasted will never be recovered. Do not do things because others are doing it. Yours might not be the same as the others. "Temptation is a woman's weapon and man's excuse" (H. L. Mencken). Therefore, fall no victim to such.

When I traveled to my village in January 2004, I found out that a good number of my high school mates had passed away as a result of sexually transmitted diseases. There should not be any reason to let careless lifestyle kill you. Educate yourself so you can know better. They always say that ignorance of the law is not an excuse. Therefore, it is your responsibility to make yourself aware of the dangers in sexual intercourse. Life has no duplicate, and a word is enough for the wise.

Weed

Marijuana, pot, ganja, grass are all classified as weed. Marijuana is the most commonly used illicit drug. Despite the study that shows that it alleviates pain, it also increases the risk of heart diseases. Have you considered the health challenges of smoking? Smoking is scientifically proven to be a leading cause of lung cancer. Smoking of cigars not only causes cancer but also can give you higher risk of emphysema and bronchitis. Cigars will rather compromise your health instead of making you rich. To me, any risk that does not have any moral or economic justification is not worth taking. When you are under the influence of some controlled substance, it brings emotional and mental imbalance. You will be hearing voices that will be telling you to do something crazy. The Newtown, Connecticut, Elementary School massacre was not carried out on that faithful morning in someone's right state of mind. The calamity took place after the perpetrator had put himself under the control of some illicit drug. No man in a clear mind would shoot and kill 20 1st graders.

Say no to bad advices; whether it is from a known person or an invisible being. Calculate the advantages and disadvantages of those habits of the three Ws so you will be able to know whether to continue or quit. **If the implication does not justify the risk, drop them and seek success.**

Is every advice a good one?

The answer is NO. It is not every advice that is good. Some of them you really have to weigh before accepting. There are different motives of advising. Some friends would advise you genuinely. Some would advise you out of jealousy. It is up to you to recall your voice of education when the bad ones come. Your voice of education (which can be your discerning spirit) is what jumps into action when a relative or a friend is advising you deceitfully. In a situation like this, what you need is your street smartness and not book smartness. Book smartness will make you pass your examinations very well, but street smartness will make you know when someone is trying to chance (take advantage of) you. We should not be ignorant of the devices of the devil. The advice of staying away from the three Ws was hypothetically tested and proven to be a good one. It might be hard to admit, but the truth thing is that your involvement in any of the three Ws will take away your blessing from God. Therefore, it is expedient to take note of their spiritual, physical, and psychological impact on you as an individual.

Here are some points to ponder

- Always consider the moral and economic justification of the things you do
- Drop the habits that make no sense to you
- Do not emulate the bad habit of others
- Do not rejoice in wrong doings
- Remain focused in your desire to attain a goal
- Use your voice of education to weigh every advice you receive, because it is not every advice that is good
- Put your voice of education to work, especially when someone is trying to outsmart (chance) you
- Do not take the advice of abstaining from the three Ws for granted.

Chapter 8
Embrace the power of the three C words

Merriam-Webster Online (2012) defined the three Cs as follows:

1. **Coordination:** The harmonious functioning of parts for effective results
2. **Cooperation:** To act together or in compliance for mutual benefit
3. **Collaboration:** To work together jointly, especially in an intellectual endeavor

Managers, stakeholders, and board of directors do put resources and efforts together to bring organizations, companies, and even friendships to a revitalized state through their collaborated strategies. Whenever there is a teamwork with regards to planning, reasoning together, and coordinating well, decision making processes do go smoother in any organization. Also when there is collaboration, cooperation, and coordination, there is always an enhanced organizational effectiveness. In other words, it brings high productivity in an organization or a company.

The collaboration of the United States Citizenship and Immigration services (USCIS) and the United States Department of Homeland Security (DHS) has so far created the best impression of planning that focuses so directly on the coordinated intelligence. This coordinated intelligence helps to track, detect, and apprehend illegal immigrants as well as those involved in terrorist activities. Risks are shared when professional entities join hands for a more productive result. It is also more efficient to use a program and innovation that has the involvement of collaborated intelligence. This idea will make a business venture a potential success because there will be reduced fear of failure. There will be a shared liability as well as increased goods and services.

Arizona Department of Corrections (ADC) operates in collaboration, cooperation, and coordination with the local police departments and Immigration and Custom Enforcement (ICE) within the state of Arizona. For example, whenever there is a transportation that involves a high risk inmate maybe to the hospital or court, there has to be a notification made to local police departments that such a transport is about to take place. They have to be alerted ahead of time, the policemen are ready for escorts and actions as needed. This process gives the correctional officers confidence for security purposes. Death row inmates have nothing to lose but the correctional officers do. So this kind of practice works the best and produces the most productive results. In any insurance business, sharing of risk minimizes indemnity and maximizes values. Take note of that if you want to achieve success. Sharing your worries with a friend should not complicate your problems, it should alleviate them. No one is indispensable in such a way that he or she can achieve success alone without collaborated efforts. "Coming together is a beginning; keeping together is progress; working together is success" (Henry Ford). Teamwork is not trying to see who will first finish a task, but putting ideas together for a positive result. If you want to achieve success, share your idea with someone (trustworthy person), put resources together and get started. Very important, do not leak a company's secret in the name of collaboration.

I have researched extensively to see if there is any successful business that does not apply collaboration, coordination, and cooperation. There is none. Even husband and wife must cooperate and coordinate before they procreate. They procreate after fertilization has taken place. Fertilization is therefore the fusion of male and female gamete to form a zygote. Zygote is the fetus that develops into a baby. Then to raise those children requires collaborated efforts. In fact, the way the world is created makes it extremely difficult for one person to succeed or even survive without the help of someone else. It is a life of symbiosis. The word "symbiosis" is a biological term that entails mutually beneficial relationship between plants and animals as well as two people or group of people. If plants and animals need one another of different species to make it; how much more human beings?

Stop running away from your peers because you need them to pass your training session at your workplace. Stop running away from your so-called enemy because you need him or her to establish that venture. A collaborated effort has never failed a company, but a detached effort has negatively impacted a company. Be wise and apply the strategies of the three C words for you will not regret. The techniques of collaboration, cooperation, and coordination will yield positive outcomes in any business.

I have come to realize that rich people alone cannot survive on earth. Therefore, the rich needs the poor in order to keep life going. There are some menial jobs the rich people cannot do and will never even venture doing, but somebody has to do them. It is a normal thing that someone will own a land, and someone else will irrigate (water) the land. On the other hand, poor people cannot survive without the rich people. **Life is balanced when the rich, the poor, and the middle class can cooperate, coordinate, and collaborate with one another.**

Republicans will cooperate with Democrats in order to see success in the white house. The House of Representatives and the Senate will somewhat come together on decisions before there is progress and unity in Congress. A student needs his teacher to succeed. I have noticed that it is hard to pass a class if you hate your teacher. *That is why it is not good to hate if you desire success.* Success comes after a harmonious collaboration of efforts and ideas. "As you navigate through the rest of your life, be open to collaboration. Other people and other people's ideas are often better than your own. Find a group of people who challenge and inspire you, spend a lot of time with them, and it will change your life" (Amy Poehler).

Are you the best or the pest?

Kevin has always been Timothy's friend right from high school. Wherever Timothy goes, Kevin goes there. Whatever Timothy does, Kevin wants to do the same thing. Kevin tries to be close-marking his friend because he believes that he gets protection staying around him. Timothy does not quite like Kevin that much due to the fact that they both do not have the same characteristics, but they hang out anyway, maybe because of the saying that opposite attracts. The only thing they have in common is competing for best grade performances in class.

Kevin takes every habit of his to the extreme, and that is what I classify as addiction. He knows no limit as in when to stop on anything. His reckless lifestyle has put him in a very bad health condition. Since Timothy is a little too conservative and very reserved a person to be hanging out with Kevin, he tried his possible best to drop the friendship but his efforts have been proven abortive. Kevin at some point is referred to as *"one week one trouble,"* he is always getting into serious troubles. In fact, he causes commotion wherever he goes. Inside the classroom he is very brilliant, but outside the classroom he is as dumb as you can never imagine. The bottom line is that Kevin really claims to be Timothy's best friend, but Timothy thinks he is a **pest**.

So as we are trying to cling unto a successful person in order to tap into success, always remember to ask yourself if you are taken as the *best friend or the pest friend* because there is a difference between best and pest, even though they both have the same vowel sounds. When you are always a parasite, it takes just a little while before your host starts reacting. Someone can condone the fact that you are struggling with habits, but to posses some parasitic behaviors on top of it, is in fact a nightmare, and may not work well with you. Know it today that a friendship cannot last if it is one sided.

Here are some points to ponder

- Apply the concepts of the three Cs in everything you do because it is very difficult to make it alone
- If you hate your teacher, you fail your class. **How is that?**
- Do not think that because you are rich, you do not need anything from anybody. It is a lie because, there is what the poor man has that you do not have. You might want to marry his beautiful daughter one day
- The success of every business is sharing of information and putting resources together
- Insurance companies succeed by sharing risks
- No man is an island, entire of itself; every man is a piece of the continent (John Donne)
- Do not be selfish in friendships.

Chapter 9
Political, Social, and Economic insights in the U. S. Government

America is a capitalist country that operates under democracy. Democracy is then addressed by the 16th president of the United States, Abraham Lincoln as the government of the people, by the people, and for the people. It is also one of the political ideologies that advocate governmental control over all sources of power. There was in the past an apparent need for a centralized governing body that should revise the article of confederation, which showed a weakness in the Congress. The United States congress was going through lack of governmental control over power at some point. Congress was not powerful enough to command respect, raise funds, and involve in foreign policies. So, there was much deliberation on the issue of the government not having common defense, security of liberty, and general welfare.

According to the library of Congress, "The Constitutional Convention of 1787 proposed a new constitution establishing a much stronger national government. Although this controversial new Constitution provoked a great deal of resistance, it was eventually ratified by the necessary number of states, replacing the Articles of Confederation as the framework of the United States government." George Washington presided over the aforementioned convention held in Philadelphia from May 25 to September 18 of the same year. This is where they vested all Legislative powers in the Congress. James Madison stated, "If men were angels, no government would be necessary." Meanwhile, men are not angels; they desire power, and if there is power to be had, someone will aspire to it. So power is necessary to get things done; too much power is corrupting because power intoxicates. They then decided to create an atmosphere where there will be separation of powers within the three branches of government; legislative, where Congress makes laws; executive, which involves the president and the cabinets; judiciary, which involves the interpretation of the law by the U. S. Supreme court. This system discouraged a tyrannical concentration of power; instead it preferred checks and balances.

The major economic predicament the new nation faced right after the world war put them at a state where bankruptcy was almost inevitable. There was much debt incurred on the national body that led to the Board of Treasury submitting a report warning that, "unless the states immediately adopted the measures recommended by Congress in 1783, nothing can rescue us from Bankruptcy, or preserve the union of the several States from Dissolution," (Library of Congress).

A similar national debt (as a result of wars; Iraq and Afghanistan) is what we are experiencing now. The present economic state of this nation has given not only the citizens concerns but also the government. The country's economic meltdown has caused people to lose their homes, jobs, vehicles, and even marriages. The federal government intervened by bringing out some strategies that helped to reduce the impact on the society. Programs like the bailout of some financial and auto companies were enacted. The government disbursed about $536,163,862,026 in the bailout of companies like: Fannie Mae, AIG, Freddie Mac, General Motors, Bank of America, Citigroup, JP Morgan Chase, Wells Fargo, GMAC, Chrysler, PNC, etc.

Cash for clunkers was also introduced as a measure to alleviate financial burden on American people. One of my friends, Horacio even took advantage of it and traded in his antique gas guzzling cars for brand new Toyota Rav4 vehicles. **You have to stay in touch and not out of touch if you want to achieve success.** This is the only way to know when they are sharing the national cake. Meanwhile, cash for clunkers was a $3 billion federal government program that intended to not only bring economic stimulus to Americans, but should also boost the economy by increasing the volume of sales of fuel efficient brand new cars.

The most troubling problem concerning the impact of war on the economy has to do with rapidly rising public debt. The social state of this nation during war has always been *fear*. People tend to worry about lives, jobs, foods, shelter, starvation, uncertainties as well as instabilities. The fear of unknown engulfed the people of the United States of America. It is one of the reasons why the constitution stipulated that on no condition should the president and commander in chief declare or wage war against any nation without the proper procedure of consulting the Congress. The Congress has to determine the necessity for war. The U. S. Constitution Article one, Section eight unambiguously gives Congress the authority to declare war.

Just because power intoxicates, everyone knows that if you give the executive led by the president full authorization to declare war, believe it or not, there will be war with this country every year. In so doing, the social wellbeing of the citizens will be deteriorating. Our men and women in battle field will be losing their sanity and mental competence due to the effect of war. There have been some touchy cases of post-traumatic stress disorder (PTSD) as a result of war. A former co-worker who had served the nation relentlessly in the battle field is not deemed competent today to still be an employee of the organization because of his PTSD status.

Immigration is a very lucrative source of federal government revenue. It has come to my understanding that the federal government of the United States cannot decide to abolish or stop admitting foreigners (immigrant and non-immigrant status) to the country. The set of people in question are those who do the dirty jobs. They go out in the rain and snow to do those things American born citizens cannot do. Overall, they help to boost the economy of the country either by trade, labor, or service. Many people have expressed their concerns over how the immigrants are taking away their jobs or causing havoc to the peace of the nation, but the United States Congress and other federal officials have realized the impact of immigration to the continued growth of the United States. For one to change status from a permanent resident to a citizen, he or she is legally required to pay nearly one thousand dollars. It is just one example of many avenues they raise money through immigration.

In every situation, America is still the land of opportunity. As a nation comprises of people from different race, color, and ethnic background, the declaration of human rights of 1948 by the United Nations has positively stood to portray freedom and equality to American people regardless of sexuality or socio-economic status. Human rights can be said to be those rights deemed necessary to have as humans, and were provided by the government for the purposes of peace, happiness, and equity.

As stated in the Universal Declaration of Human Rights, "Everyone has the right to life, liberty and security of person." I believe that it is a good thing to appreciate the fact that we should not take the things we have for granted. Everyone wants to come and settle here in the United States because of the rights and liberties we have.

There was a trip I made back in 2000. When I came back from that trip, which was nothing to write home about, I stood right in front of my apartment in Irvington, New Jersey and said God bless America as I kissed the ground. **I will forever appreciate the orderliness and peacefulness of this great nation**. The organized transportation system, the adequate education system, and the remarkable job opportunities in this country can never be underestimated. What about the cleanliness of the environment? It is amazing to learn that you really do not have to have too much money in your pocket to get as many degrees as you want. In other words, if you cannot pay now, you can pay later. I will always advise people to make haste while the sun shines. Take advantage of the opportunity you have when you can. When you know the political, social, and economic activities of this country, you are close to achieving success. The knowledge of American government will guide you into realizing what is right and wrong. When you know your right from your left, you are a mile closer to achieving success.

Here are some points to ponder

- Ignorance of the law is not an excuse; therefore, know your government as you are searching for success
- Power is good but it intoxicates. Excessive use of power is bad
- The economic standing of any nation depends on its political stability
- War does more harm/damage than good.
- We should not take for granted what we have
- Recognize the fact that both immigrants and the natives of America are here for one common goal.
- Stay in touch so you won't be left behind
- Be aware of your surrounding so you know when they are sharing the national cake

Chapter 10
Things you should not do if you want to achieve success

- Do not be lazy
- Do not be afraid to fail
- Do not envy
- Do not compromise
- Do not be despondent
- Do not be extravagant

Do not be lazy

When your desire has always been to be successful, and you cannot wake up in a cold winter morning to go to work, it is hard to make it. Even if you desire to have your own business, and you still cannot wake up in the morning to go out, you will find it difficult to make ends meet. Manners will never fall from heaven. The hand work of an industrious man yields dividend in the end. In everything you do, put energy to it. Sleep no more and get to work. You keep procrastinating over the idea of going to school. Just do it today and increase your chances of succeeding in life. *You have evidently done the procrastination for too long. Do your part and leave the rest to God.*

You keep putting off the desire to get a job. Just go out there and search for jobs. If you send out one hundred resumes in a month, at least one will click. If you are always tired, when will you be strong to seek success? There is absolutely no reason for one to wake up in the morning after eight hours of sleep and complain, "Oh I am so tired today." You have not even done anything. "The sluggard craves and gets nothing, but the desires of the diligent are fully satisfied" (Proverbs 13:4).

Explore your options when you are still young, because it might be too late when you are old. I am glad that I was able to travel to **Amsterdam, Holland; Hamburg, Germany; Munich, Germany; Paris, France; New York, U. S. A. and London, United Kingdom** when I did it because traveling is part of education. No exposure is a waste. I found out that as long as we are alive, we will keep learning new things, and there are many things you learn from meeting new people from another culture. My ability to travel around the western world has created uncountable opportunities for me.

Do not be afraid to fail

You should not be afraid to start new things. Many a time we worry about what people will say if we fail, and in so doing, we deny ourselves the chance to succeed. How are you going to succeed if you are afraid to try that venture? The answer is that you cannot succeed if you do not try. Your inability to start that project that you have been longing for has deterred your ability to become a *millionaire*.

If Thomas Edison who invented light bulb after many attempts was afraid of failure, he would not have succeeded in becoming the fourth most prolific inventor in history. If you are willing to achieve success, do not be afraid to fail. Fear of failure or fear of unknown is an excuse of a lazy man. There is absolutely no reason for you not to try as much as you can to improve your worth. Your senators and governor are not smarter than you are. So why should you be afraid of success.

Even a so called 'gang banger' in New York City turned himself into a rapper after the death of his mother. Today, his fame knows no bound. He is successful as a singer. I went to Germany back in 2003 and the German people who would not understand English under normal circumstances were there singing and dancing his song. He is known worldwide. Remember he is from the street. That is what I call success. It is okay if you were born with silver spoon in your mouth, but what impresses me more is when you make it from nowhere, but out of your own determination. Do not be afraid to fail because failure strengthens your desire to succeed.

Do not envy

This is a strong commandment that we tend to overlook often times. Try not to slander a successful person out of envy. Neither should you try to wish your girlfriend death only because she got married before you. Also it is not morally right to start telling people that your girlfriend was the one who proposed to a man instead of the other way round. Do not wish to possess your neighbor's possessions, including his wife. Where will your neighbor be when you are living your dream of taking all that belongs to him? Obviously, you want him dead or imprisoned because your dream would not come to pass while he is still around. Be happy when your friend is happy. Weep when your friend is in agony. After weeping with her, you encourage her to move on. Envy brings jealousy and covetousness. "**Thou shalt not covet** thy neighbor's house, thou shalt not covet thy neighbor's wife, nor his manservant, nor his maidservant, nor his ox, nor his ass, nor any thing that is thy neighbor's" (Exodus 20).

Do not compromise

When you work in an organization where it is unethical to show personal favors to the people you have care or custody over (for example, patients or inmates), how firm can you be? It might be morally right to exchange gifts with these categories of individuals but ethically wrong. Therefore, it is strongly recommended to abide by the code of conduct of your company or organization which stipulates the zero tolerance policy in doing such favors. In a special case like this, you will have to leave that which is morally right and do that which is ethically right in order to maintain your integrity and professionalism. If you are too kind to be in a particular field, leave and look for another career. No success will come if you compromise and lose your job or go to jail for breaking the law.

When I first started working for the Department of Corrections (DOC) back in 2006, I had an opportunity to be part of a transport team that would escort an inmate to a hospital. The first question my supervisor asked me was, "Are you afraid to shoot?" My answer was no. People might see it as meanness. He was not being mean to the inmate or me, but only wanted to make sure; because if the inmate attempts to escape, you will not have any option but to shoot. The point is that if you are afraid to shoot, you are in the wrong field. If you have a reason to shoot and refused to shoot, you have compromised.

There are many reasons why people compromise. People compromise due to fear. People compromise due to self-interest. If you are selfish, you are vulnerable. Meanwhile, vulnerability exposes one to danger. In your dealings with people; be fair, firm, and consistent so that justice will always take its place.

Justice in general is fairness. However, in every fairness of justice, there is distributive justice, and justice as a virtue. While discussing the concept of justice, it is important to know the reason why offenders or perpetrators are punished. They are punished because you want to bring them to justice. Here, bringing one to justice is giving the person an appropriate penalty based on the offense committed. "An ethic of justice and rights tells us to regulate our actions or lives in accordance with certain general moral principles" (Plato). As justice deals with fairness to a person, social equity deals with fairness in the delivery of public services. Therefore, these two concepts go together as in promoting fairness and freedom in the society. It is therefore required of you to treat people with fairness regardless of their social status; even if the person is a prisoner. In any situation, do not cross boundary. If you cross the boundary, you have compromised. If you compromise, you will face the consequences.

Do not be despondent

Do not give up and do not lose hope. If you are sick, you need to tell yourself that you will be fine. If you are looking for a life partner, do not stop because God has not stopped with you. If you have failed in many businesses, do not quit trying. Eventually, you will get it. See yourself as an optimistic person and believe that there is hope. You should never believe that you will ever fail. That is what is expected of every human being. Optimism is antonymous with despondency and pessimism. Meanwhile, despondency is a strong hold that is contrary to positive mindedness. Optimism is a positive attitude that keeps telling you that you will accomplish a certain goal. You know that there are chances that you might not succeed doing something, but that urge to try it anyway is called optimism. That is what you need. Conquer despondency and pursue your desire for success. With despondency you see no hope in life. You lack the desire to work hard. **You despise the call for glorious adventures**.

If you are a man and willing to get married, but you are waiting until you have money so you can do that. Who told you that you do not have money? Tell the voice that is putting the negative thought in you to get behind you because it is the spirit of despondency. In your twenties, you did not have money. In your thirties, you did not have money. In your forties, you still did not have money. Have you not already realized that you are being deceived? *Say no to pessimism* and make that bold step into success. As soon as you conquer that fear, you will witness the joy of success. Success comes with "practicality."

If you have failed out of school many times, you should go back because you have not graduated. Going back is nobody else's business but yours. If you do not feel like telling anyone this time around, it is okay but just go back.

Do not be extravagant

Being extravagant does not mean that you have to be stingy, but you need to be prudent. You cannot make eight hundred dollars a month and use five hundred on fast food and other habits of yours. The remaining three hundred will not even pay your bills for the month not to talk of saving some. If you eat out every day, there is no way you can make ends meet, especially when you are a low income earner. It is arithmetically impossible. Cut your coat according to your size. Be wise in spending. **Women**, do not get me wrong; it is different from being cheap. When you are wise in spending, you buy things that you need and not things that you want. When you like everything you see at the stores and on television commercials, you must always be in want. In today's materialistic world, we really need to exercise fiscal discipline. If not, you will put yourself in so much debt that God Himself cannot deliver you from it.

In East Coast, I have met a woman who writes down every penny she spends. It is not because Carmen is a Certified Public Accountant (CPA), but because she wants to make sure she does not spend more than what she makes. It is so easy to go over your income, especially in today's world of credit cards. That is why she tracks her daily expenses. At the end of the month, she reconciles her account. There should be no reason why you will be spending more than what you earn. If that is your case, well something is wrong somewhere. You might want to seek a professional advice. Success is wisdom. Carmen's wisdom of setting her daily spending limit paid back. Today, she is very prosperous. She has attained financial freedom just for being smart with her money. The above listed six things (laziness, fear, envy, compromise, despondency, and extravagance) are detrimental to our ability to succeed.

Here are some points to ponder

- There are too many things you are legally permitted to do, but there are also things you should not do because they are not morally acceptable
- Spend wisely because you do not know tomorrow
- Lazy people are incompetent because they lack the zeal to succeed
- There is a price you pay when you compromise
- Do not eat like a glutton but at the same time, do not be stingy
- By all means, try to be creative in life because there is a reward for productivity.

Chapter 11
Doing the right thing with the wrong motive

There is always a motive behind every deed of men. What is your motive in life? <u>Self-interest</u> is a motive. <u>Financial freedom</u> is a motive as well as <u>public service</u>. It is therefore your sole responsibility to make sure that your motive is a genuine one. It has been discovered that bad or rather wrong motives are always capable of bringing regrets. I would not want to engage in activities that will eventually result to regrets.

Self Interest

Napoleon has a Bachelor's degree in Criminal Justice. He got a job working for the United States Department of Justice. It is a federal job one can call a career and build his future around it. Instead Napoleon one day called his wife and said to her, "I think I am going to go back to school for nursing." His wife knows too well that he cannot stand blood not to talk of messing with so many other nauseating things you see in a nursing profession. So, his wife disagreed with him and told him plainly that his sudden interest in nursing was not because he wanted to save lives, but because of "money."

Being a registered nurse is a good thing, but if you do it without any compassion whatsoever; rather to make the so-called "big money" like others. It is a wrong motive. If you practice medicine without having the love to save lives, you will end up killing the people you are supposed to be saving. Check your motive; make sure it is in line with your personality and capability. You ought to have a genuine interest in the things you do in order to do them right. Napoleon went for his Master's degree rather, and today he enjoys what he does. Thank God for his wife who told him the truth.

Financial Freedom

A highly regarded Wall Street businessman, William was doing so well financially. He had a mansion in his New York home. He had a Rolls Royce car and multiple other luxury cars as well as a private jet. He lived in New York, but was also in law school at one of the universities in United Kingdom. William had opened a company and was selling shares to Americans in America's largest stock exchange market. The investors, shareholders, and stakeholders were ignorantly investing their wealth in a bogus company of his. Everything looked too good to be true, but people still could not read in between the lines. A good number of Americans fell victims of his scam. The presentation of his company was full of false information.

The owner of the bogus company wanted financial freedom by all means so he disregarded the power of trust and embraced the power of wealth. He became too materialistic in such a way that he started drawing attention to himself.

Even though he made too much wealth fraudulently, but he ended up in prison for over than 10 years now. Not only that he is serving time in the federal prison, but all he had acquired were also confiscated by the government. Many lives were ruined due to this ruthless act. Some people committed suicide after they learned that all their investments/shares were put in a never existed stock market. If you invest in stock and market crashes, it is bearable, but if you invest money and later realized that the stock never even existed, it is heartbreaking and a dangerous crime against humanity. We live in the most sophisticated part of the world, so our desire for success should and must be with caution. Use your intelligence to create something beneficial to all concerned.

Public Service

Have you ever appreciated the services of the Firefighters, Correctional Officers, Police Officers, and our Military men and women? These are the people who do public service duties for our freedom, security, and protection. They protect the nation against external invaders and other national threats. They defend our country. They also provide security and peace to American citizens. They put their lives on the line for us and for our country.

Janice Brewer, the governor of Arizona said that in her effort to cut budget in this time of economic crunch that she could not afford to neglect our public safety jobs. They are jobs that cannot be compromised with despite the effort to have a balanced budget.

I had the opportunity to come in contact with late Charles Browning who once told me, "I do this job for the fun of it and not for the money." He was a Correctional Officer who devoted his time being the best officer he could be at Arizona Department of Corrections (ADC). His efforts to carry out the correctional duties of ADC with so much enthusiasm and determination were not proven abortive (not in vain) as one of the correctional facilities was named after him when this diligent young American soldier later got killed in Afghanistan by an explosion of improvised electronic device (IED). It was in him I saw the true spirit of public service. He used his strength and intelligence to defend and to correct notwithstanding the pay (money).

A public service worker does not consider himself first, rather the public. The motive behind the job of a public service man is to protect you from danger. There was a fire in a New York home. The very first two responders were killed. They were not killed by fire, but by the owner of the house who set his house on fire and waited for the public service workers to arrive to their deaths. He wrote down on a piece of paper, "Let me do what I enjoy doing." Always pray for these categories of people who put their lives in danger in order to provide safety, security, and protection for you. While your motive is to make money, some people's motives are to save you even if it takes sacrificing their lives.

Whatever you do, respect your job and put in your best to it. Like what you do and enjoy your performance. Do it with passion and diligence. Tim was a car salesman at Metro Honda, Jersey City, New Jersey. Phil came to him and said, "Tim please I want you to help me get a job at your workplace." Tim has flourished doing this job so he has already built a reputation. The more you sell, the more money you make. Tim helped Phil to get the job, but unfortunately it was not what Phil anticipated. His expectation was to sit in an office, dressed in suit and money would be coming. So when he realized that you actually need to work hard to sell one car, he became frustrated. Every day Phil would complain to Tim, "I really do not like *this **your** job. This **your*** job is crazy." At a point Tim got tired of hearing the whining about what has suddenly become his job, he had to put a stop to Phil's endless complaints. He did not want Phil's negative attitude to affect him. So Tim advised him to resign and continue looking for what he could do and enjoy doing. Phil left the job and continued his search for success, but success comes easier with a genuine motive.

What is your motive behind rendering a helping hand to others? Do you do it for the whole world to notice, or do you do things so that you can take advantage of the person you are supposed to be helping? Abayomi is an African immigrant who came to the United States to live American dream just like every other person. He joined his roommate working for Amoco gas station in Hasbrouck Heights, New Jersey. Abayomi wanted to get another job that he could be doing during the day. He had no car yet. So he figured that since his roommate has only one job which they both go at night that getting a day time job would not be a bad idea. Abayomi asked his roommate if it was okay to use his car as he wished to start a second job. His roommate said, "Sure why not." Abayomi went to Sentinel Security Services and got hired instantly to start working the next day. He came home and told his roommate that he got a job. He was happy for him. When the time came for Abayomi to go to work, his roommate told him to cooperate if he wanted to take the car. Be advised Abayomi is a guy and his roommate is also a guy. As he was wandering what kind of cooperation his roommate was talking about; his roommate specified that he should take off his clothes. His motive was to take advantage of Abayomi because he did not have a car. The young newly immigrated African fled for his life and sanity. He packed out of the studio apartment without any prior notice. Even though this man had also used Abayomi's personal information to obtain a credit card, forged his signatures and cashed his check, but the law of karma has caught up with him. He is now serving time in prison somewhere in Georgia for different other reasons. You cannot take advantage of a handicap and expect success.

Chen is a registered nurse from Philippines. She got married to Brad because she wanted to go to America. She never considered the fact that Brad was 20 years older than she was. She just wanted to get her papers first. She came to America and was being in her best behavior until after she got her citizenship. She classified her husband as one with bipolar. Not only that she diagnosed him of being mentally challenged, she also realized that he was 20 years older. Chen started going to movie theaters by herself without telling her husband. She started leaving work so early to hang out while in the pretense of still at work. One day, Brad brought lunch to her at work, and he was told that Chen had already left for the day. He went home and Chen was not home. He called Chen, but Chen could not answer her phone instead she sent him a text message that she was busy at work; that she would get off at 4:00 pm. Meanwhile, she did not know that Brad had already been at her workplace at 1:40 pm. She started lying to her husband to cover her crooked ways. She made her motive for marrying Brad a top secret. Today, the marriage is over, but Brad is not dead yet of his mental illness.

If you ever leave your spouse and start going to restaurants and movies alone, you are making yourself vulnerable and available. You know pretty sure that you are not Jesus. So what makes you think that you are capable of resisting temptations? If you can leave work and go straight to a man's house so as to settle a dispute he has with his wife and in the absence of the man's wife, your motive is wrong, different, and suspicious. "A wise woman builds her home, but a foolish woman tears it down with her own hands" (Proverbs 14:1). What are the motives behind you getting married to the person you got married to? Are you looking for money, America, or love? Lean not unto your own understanding because there is a way that seemeth right unto man, but the end of it is destruction.

If your spouse is in desperate need of money, and you have it but will never give him or her, you have the wrong motive. If your husband lost his job, and you turned back at him immediately after all "he is supposed to be the provider," you have lost the meaning of marriage in your dictionary. Get it right! These are the principles that should guide you as you look into the motives behind all of your actions. If your spouse cannot drive your car, who can?

Angel got married to a dentist. The husband bought a new Mercedes car that was his 'personal toy.' Angel was never allowed access to the Mercedes car. She continued being cool, calm, and collected until the day she saw her sister in-law driving that same car that she never was allowed to use; that was the day Angel lost her temper and broke all the breakables. When you got married to your spouse, you signed to tolerate and to condone. If you cannot do that today you need to rediscover your motive.

Here are some points to ponder

- There is no good benefit in doing things with an ulterior motive

- Get a job that you know you can do so you will not have any reason not to do it well
- Do not forget that we live in a sophisticated world where things are detected easier than you think
- Try not to fool yourself at the end of the day when you think you are fooling someone else
- Share with your spouse what you have because one plus one is equal to one
- Do not try to look good outside, but in the house you are very bad
- That Mercedes car that you do not want your wife to ever touch, if a co-worker asks you to use it for an errand, won't you give him or her?
- In your attempt to make wealth, do not do it at the detriment of others
- You cannot take advantage of a handicap and expect success.

Chapter 12
What goes around comes around

It is expedient to live a life that is worthy of emulation. Think about how many times you have ganged up against your friend or rather a fellow human being. Consider the outcome of it. Did your intention for such materialize? Did the outcome justify what you went through in this plot? One Frank had once said "I do not want any war because if it starts, people will start dying." In other words, "when it rains it pours." The effect of war affects all regardless of your socio-economic status. That is why J. P. Clark expressed in his poem, *The Casualties,* that the casualties are not only those who are dead, they are well out of it; and the casualties are not only those who are wounded in the war, though they await burial by installment. When you wage war against a nation or a family, you will definitely receive a glimpse of the effect of war no matter how protected you are. You can wear bullet proof vest all day long, build a bunker and hide in it; when your home is demolished, you are automatically affected even though you survived death.

The assurance we are getting from this is that whatever

we do in the dark must surely come to light. If our plots are for good, goodness and mercies shall follow us all the days of our lives. But if our plots are evil, the wicked shall never rule the land of the righteous. The evil that men do lives with them. It might take a while before it gets to you, but slowly and surely it will come. People kill not only with sword or by shooting, but with words of mouth. You will be judged by what proceeds out of your mouth. "Not that which goeth into the mouth defileth a man; but that which cometh out of the mouth, this defileth a man" (Matthew 15:11). Your kindness unto another is what gives you joy. He who has joy is already enjoying the joy of success. After all, what else is success? *Success is joy.*

If your job is to always gather with your kind and condemn, you need to have a **remorseful** and **repentant** heart so you can embrace joy. Life is too short for you to remain antagonistic. This is exactly when poverty crawls in. Anyone with vision and ambition has no time for unproductive act because he or she is looking forward to accomplishing either a short term or a long term goal.

Davis was a sanitary prefect (school official) at Comprehensive Secondary School, Nawfia, Nigeria. He hated John's gut with passion. Davis used his authority as a senior student to deal with John so mercilessly. He was always punishing John for no reason. He would deny John his rights and freedom. He literally controlled John's happiness throughout his tenure of office. The repercussion fell on Davis when he performed poorly on his exams, and that denied him the opportunity to go to the next grade. John got promoted to even a higher post. Even though he did not retaliate against Davis, but he used his high position and authority bestowed on him as the deputy senior prefect to put Davis in place.

It should not come to you as a surprise that Davis not only got demoted, but also he was caught stealing and selling students' mattresses. After going through the usual torture and humiliation, Davis learned not to be wicked to anyone whether he likes the person or not. Here Davis voiced, "I will never forget the day I was humiliated by my inferiors." That statement does not matter anymore; what matters is that *what goes around comes around.*

I personally like to keep track of events because they serve as a guide for me. I learn from the happenings of time gone by. Experience is not just learning from your mistakes, but acquiring knowledge from what goes on around you.

Joyce got married to her soul mate (a medical doctor) after graduating from law school. They were happily married even though there have not been any children for about six years of marriage. She never relented on her kind works to people. She had organized baby shower parties for many other women. She ignored her condition of not having any kids of her own and continued with her good heart; heart of kindness and favor. As God would have it, He remembered that Joyce has been helpful to the needy. She was blessed with three children in three years. As if that blessing was not enough, she got a lucrative job to be teaching in a law school.

It is expedient to sow the right seeds so that the hard labor of your youth days will pay off in the end. The trophies you accumulated in your active days will worth much when you need them the most. The joy of every man is to be able to look back someday and say "Thank God for all the accomplishments." This is what I call ***The Joy of Success.***

I am a player

Venus was a young and beautifully made girl who almost believed that the world was a bed of roses. She grew up in a suburb of Somerset, New Jersey where she enjoyed life to the fullest. She not only loved hanging out but she also could dance so attractively. Wherever it was happening, she was there. She had everything she needed as in house, food, and money to satisfy her obsession for materialistic pleasures.

At a point, Venus became too full of herself to the extent of proudly calling herself **a player**. She believed that if she is out to a party with her girlfriends, that all attention will always be given to her. She then saw it as an advantage to get any man she wanted. She kept getting different versions of men; the good, the bad, and the ugly. Despite her privilege of getting almost everything she needed from her parents, which includes but not limited to tuition, medical care, a car, clothes, high end cell phones, her desire for a rich man was ceaseless.

In the process of searching for a rich man, Venus missed a successful man. In her area, there were too many rich men, but one successful man. **The heart of a successful man is peace and love with vision and ambition**; but in her dictionary, success is driving of Escalade.

As Venus was traveling all around the country in search of this faceless rich man, she built a reputation. The reputation was a very hard one to eradicate. She graduated from college and obtained her Bachelor's degree but still was unable to find her imaginary soul mate. As the clock was ticking, her friends were getting married, and she was aging. She figured that this is no more time for **dazzling** and **tantalizing**. She had no choice at this time but to go make a lifetime investment (marriage commitment) on what my late father, J. U. Okafor used to call a blind alley. "So since it is such a big deal getting a self-made man, let me go and get the one I can make," Venus voiced.

My mother, Ngozi Okafor used to tell me that a cheater must be cheated. In this case, **a player has been played**. It is either you make a man or you break a man. In Venus attempt to make this man that she really invested much on, she ended up breaking him. And that was the end of the marriage. Try to make sure that your understanding of success is in accordance with its actual meaning. If you define something (success) the way it will suit you, when alarm blows, you face the consequences.

"Whenever I allowed my subconscious mind to stray back into the happenings of time gone by, I could not help but remembered this particular incident which did not only dig a permanent hole in my heart, but also taught me a lesson, which has driven me through trial in this world of confusion. If I had anticipated or prognosticated what would happen between me and my long awaited husband, I would have avoided the mistake and just settle with a promising lad who has now become indomitable," said Venus.

Here are some points to ponder

- Treat people with love and respect because respect is reciprocal
- Despise nobody because you do not know who will be the leaders of tomorrow
- Grab the right man when you see him because good men are hard to find

- Do not call yourself a player because one day, a player must be played
- Do not misuse your opportunity because a wasted time can never be recovered
- Do not use your position to take advantage of others.
- You will be judged by what you say. In other words, it is good to know that you have the right to remain silent because anything you say can easily be used against you.

Chapter 13
Testimonial Statements

"I was living in Los Angeles. Had a great job at 40 and was not putting one penny away in savings. I was spending money faster than I was making it, living the single life. I knew every bar and restaurant along Hollywood Boulevard, and bartenders and waitresses knew me by name.

Now I'm living a comfortable retirement. What turned me around?

Reality. I noticed my co-workers and friends moving on with their lives. While I was stuck in a small apartment, they were getting married, buying homes and establishing a life beyond the nightclub. I knew I had to get serious and start saving.

I tore up all of my 13 credit cards

At the time I owed over $30,000 in credit card bills and my interest was over 19% on each card. Each card had a limit of $10,000. I cut them all up and started using a debit card.

I got on a budget

I created a budget. I paid off several cards in two years and reduced my expenses and saved over $900 a month. My income was $40,000 a year I was 40 which was a net of around $2,500 month. However, I charged everything. When I tore up my credit cards I put myself on strict budget: rent $440 per month, car note $275, and credit card $400 a month. I took all the extra cash and paid off my lowest balance credit card first, then second. I also put over 20% of my gross into the 401(k) and profit sharing programs and stock options at work.

I took advantage of my company's profit sharing and 401(k) options

Before I was 40, I never put any money away into our company's saving programs. I started putting the highest percentage allowable of my salary into the company's profit sharing and 401(k) program. Working for ABM (American Building Maintenance) I was also able to purchase stock at an employee discount rate of 20%, so I added that to my nest egg.

I purchased rental property

At 40, I was able to purchase my first rental property in Pennsylvania for $8,000. With my wife we paid cash for the house. As an old Victorian home split into three apartments it grosses over $1,500 a month. Within a few years, I built our rental income to over $85,000 a year including selling a few properties at a profit.

I married well

Bef0ore I turned 40 I had never been married, but meeting my wife was my best decision ever. My wife is thrifty and our combined incomes were well over $100,000 a year. With her spendthrift abilities we were able to pay off all of our credit card debts.

Being married to the right person with the same mindset has been my best investment by far.

We hired a financial advisor

We hired an expert to look at our plans for retiring when we were in our mid-fifties. She calculated our money and life goals, living expenses, health plans, and our level of risk. Her advice helped us build our stock and other investment income to prepare for retirement.

We were moderately aggressive investors and with her advice -- along with our international equities and other investments -- were able to build up a very good nest egg.

We downsized

In 2006, we downsized and sold our home in Pasadena, Calif. along with a few of our rental properties and moved to a less expensive area in the Republic of Panama. Between the current market and our pension, dividends, and rental income of about $70,000 per year, we are now retired and living comfortably within our means, with expenses that total only $34,000 per year." by Augustine St. Claire.

"I define success as the attainment of one desired goal. To attain success, one has to have a plan; this plan can be short term or long term depending on the scope of work, the amount of effort, and the time it takes to accomplish the set goal.

I decided very early in life that I wanted to be an electrical engineer. I knew this was not going to come easy but was ready to do whatever it takes to attain this goal. I remember joining a science club back in high school and being kicked out from the club due to my falling grade. As faith would have it, I got another opportunity to follow my dream when I migrated to the United States, and I took full advantage of it.

I cannot count the number of times I have fallen in the course of attaining this goal, but one thing I do know is this, I got brighter and better after each fall. The word "**quit**" does not exist as far as I am concerned. I live by the Bible verse from Philippians 4:13 that states "I can do all things through Christ that gives me strength." I have never been afraid to fall and I am where I am today due to God's mercy and favor and also due to **my resilient attitude towards life**.

I always pray before embarking on a project, because I know that it is God that gives victory at the end of the day and not man."

By *Engr. **Charles Aguwamba***

"Success is always defined by all differently. From my perspective, it is what brings those who embrace it fulfillment, contentment and happiness. For those who pursue it, success becomes the motivating factor. No matter how it is defined, success brings us joy and a very fulfilling end in our quest for a lasting peace of mind. The road to achieving success can be varied and daunting. As a student, it meant working hard for good grades, which would ultimately help me land a good job upon graduation. As a professional, success involves managing and maneuvering all the nuances of the corporate world to achieve and sustain an enduring career.

However, the reality was a different case in my experience. It meant constantly confronting teachers that challenged my work, even when I was convinced that such scrutinizing was unnecessary. Nevertheless, with hard work, perseverance, and belief in my capabilities, all these came to pass. During those trying periods, I never entertained any thoughts of **quitting**. Rather, I believed those obstacles were preparing me for greater challenges in the future.

After school, we still face other challenges within our jobs, families, and other extra-curricular activities that occupy our time. The best part is that the challenges of yesteryear laid a great foundation for all the successes I enjoy today: **a successful career and a great family**.

How we achieve success is always dependent on the goal that is to be achieved. But, almost always, achieving success in anything involves **hard work, dedication and sacrifices**. For many, it may come in a single try. For others, this success happens after numerous trials. In the end, it is worth every bit of those sacrifices. For me, that is the joy of success."

By *Simon Okuagu, PHARM.D*
Pharmacy Manager/Community Leader

Mr. Okafor, I commend you for your excellence in writing the book *"The Joy of Success"*.

In all cultures, the word success has endless meanings and interpretations, but has the same end result of accomplishing a goal. Success can be defined in an elementary language as simple as setting a goal and achieving such a goal. Regardless of how one or an entity achieves such accomplishment, success does not come without any hindrances or failures.

The sole source of achieving success is embedded in determination and continues its focus on visioning the positive gratification that will come with it. Success comes in various ways and types; and it can be a self or team accomplishment. It can also be inherited in terms of financial success. However, Success is not endless when achieved but rather requires continuous structured formalities to maintain the status of such success. The most satisfying success is the self or team accomplishment which comes mostly from Goal setting, planning, and execution.

The word success means achieving every element of a good life: God's salvation, Good health, prosperity, freedom of living without enemies, and a chance to give back. Have I achieved success? Yes, few I have inherited, but many I have self accomplished. Yet, maintaining such successes are challenges of formalities that have come with obstacles and breakdowns. In all, I do count my blessings each day as I give all glory to God.

I inherited success of being born in a well disciplined family and being cared for financially until I was able to care for myself. I left the country of my origin (Nigeria) to be educated in the USA. I first arrived in Phoenix, Arizona in 1984 and never left the state. Prior to departing from Nigeria, my goal was to pursue a Business Degree and return to Nigeria for my own business. In all, I developed a strong "dream for success." I began the real journey of my dream for success by enrolling in Phoenix College. Just like most young foreigners, many of us came to the United States and never wanted to go back home after learning how promising life could be in this county. Knowing that the country could be the Promised Land of many people, I made a decision to seek becoming a permanent resident of the United States as part of my goal.

Right from my childhood, it had always been a dream of mine to be self employed after College. As I got closer to graduating, I realized that a B.S. degree in Management alone is not a sufficient tool for gaining high paying employment and to start a business. The first concept I had to be successful in was to "dream big" and believe that with hard work, anyone can achieve the success of the American dream.

To achieve the "American dream" is an imposition of an acute obstacle. While I was in college, I was doing various odd jobs: dishwasher, laundry boy, etc. After four years of college I earned a B.S. degree in Management. My job skills did not seem like much of a positive change beyond the odd jobs that I was used to. Despite all that, I still wanted a successful Business. But at very least it requires trade skill and money to start a Business. The reality of becoming successful now begins with the following obstacles:

Obstacle 1. I wanted to start my own business, but I have zero funds.

Obstacle 2. I wanted to start my own business, but I have no professional skill.

Obstacle 3. I wanted to assimilate myself into the western culture after being told many times that being black is a serious handicap and a good tool for business failure in the USA. Being told that my background, coupled with a heavy accent, is inferior to what is needed and a destination for failure.

Obstacle 4: I was advised that the best bet to be near financial success would be by having three or four full time jobs paying minimum wage. At the time minimum wage was about $3.35 an hour. Therefore, if I had four full time jobs, I would be making $13.40 an hour, all jobs combined. To have this many jobs, I would be a walking dead man. So, that happened not to be the best advice to achieve my dream of success.

I regarded all the obstacles as issues that I must overcome to become successful. My first step was to research which business I can start with a little or no money, and may require no or very limited skills. I turned all obstacles into challenging goals, and formed the company BIO-JANITORIAL SERVICE, INC. in 1990. Yet, every business requires some skills and money regardless of the type of business. My capital to start this business was $200.00 which came from my savings and borrowing from family. I invested in equipment (one vacuum cleaner) and supplies (one gallon of multipurpose cleaner and one gallon of glass cleaner). The rest of supplemented supplies came from my household. I was operating with limited skills and without most of the necessary supplies of the trade.

This is all I know about Janitorial business:

A) There are too many cleaning companies in Arizona.

B) Arizona is growing and so are the buildings, which require maintenance

C) If there is no future in janitorial, how come there are so many of them?

D) The owners of the successful cleaning companies only have one head, two eyes, two ears, and two hands like me. If they can do it, I can too!

I was acting in the capacity of janitor, sales person, supervisor, and manager. Revenues of a few hundred dollars per month were derived from subcontracting work in Phoenix, Arizona. I actively started pursuing direct contracts. The first contract secured was with Superlite Block of Phoenix, Arizona. Then in 1991 was Williams Detroit Diesel of Phoenix, Arizona. During that year with a few additional new clients, BIO hired their first employee. In the years of 1992 through 1995, BIO branched out from general office cleaning to medical facilities, high-tech buildings, and manufacturing plants. In June 1993, BIO became a corporation in the state of Arizona. BIO today is listed as one of the top 25 on *The List of Janitorial Firms*, published by The Business Journal in the industry. Then I developed a unique Quality Assurance Program, based on site-defined specifications mixed with **honesty** and **integrity** to provide a cost effective service, clean and safe working environment. 1996 turned the corner for BIO with their first large contract with one of Motorola's sites, now called General Dynamics. We grew to 50 employees and grossed annual revenues of $800,000. To comply with this contract and reduce obstacles of employee turnover, BIO developed an EEO/Affirmative Action Program, a safety program. We began background investigations and drug testing. We offered above industry wages and a full range of employee benefits including health insurance, paid vacations, and a 401(K)-Retirement plan. In 1997 the company acquired several prominent clients boosting the employee roster and gross revenues. Our aspiration was to continue to have moderate growth while providing our clients the service they deserved.

Bio Janitorial Service, Inc. became a reputable and diversified facility maintenance company with a mission to provide a sanitary, clean, safe, pleasant, and healthy environment to various organizations both locally and on national levels. From a mere dream of success, the company has grown to encompass a broad spectrum of clients and offers various facility maintenance services.

I am driven by setting a goal in order to achieve success. Many have achieved success; I have achieved success, you can achieve success too. Success is a God given opportunity made for all mankind, regardless of one's background and race. It comes in various forms and ways, depending on your definition. The only meter of measurement success is your goal(s) and interpreting how well you accomplished those Goals. I have achieved what success means to me.

By **Oliver Ibeh,**
CEO Bio Janitorial Services, Inc.

Acknowledgement

I thank God who made it possible for me to start and complete my first book, *The Joy of Success*. I cannot finish the book without remembering the support I received from my wife, Linda I. Okafor and the children; Uche, Jessica, and David. I appreciate every bit of their help. Whenever I am tired of writing, my wife would say, "Just keep writing." Her words of encouragement kept me going because it was not an easy task. My first child, Uche Okafor would be introducing some sense of humor in the middle of serious concentration. Of course, I needed all that in order to keep writing. They say "all work and no play makes Jack a dull boy." It was indeed a big help. I appreciate them.

My mother, Ngozi Okafor who was an Elementary Schoolteacher before her retirement happened to be around during this time of my first book writing. I give her a big credit for not only taking care of my children when I was in graduate school, but also she gave me some meaningful ideas when I started writing 'The Joy of Success.' I stand today on the foundation laid by my parents, Chief and Mrs. J. U.

Okafor. So the credit of being where I am does not belong to me; otherwise, I am being an ingrate.

I also express my profound gratitude to my friends who participated in one way or another to make this piece of work an accomplished goal. It will be unfair to finish this book without mentioning Mrs. Ogochukwu Nwosu, the person who actually triggered my thought to start writing the book. She might be far all the way in New Jersey, but she stands as a strong pillar behind my conviction to write.

I am mightily favored to have the best colleagues at work. Their individual supports helped me so immensely to bringing my book to a conclusion. These special individuals I met at my new position at work all made my life so much easier. The fact that they treat me with kindness, respect, and love influenced my decision on selecting the title of my book. I can proudly say that I am blessed to have people who make my job easy for me. I cannot ask for better colleagues. May God bless you all.

About the Author

Tochukwu O. Okafor received his Master's degree in Public Administration with specialization in law and Public Policy from Walden University, Minneapolis, Minnesota. He has been working for State of Arizona since 2006. He currently manages the programs of Arizona Department of Corrections. He got married at the age of 29 to Linda Okafor, and their union is blessed with three children; Uchenna, Jessica, and David.

He detached from his twin sister, Chinwe Mbaneme at a very early stage in life to pursue success. It was not an easy separation for him, but he realized that the love of a family is complete when there is success. After all, success is capable of reuniting people once again. He is a member of American Society for Public Administration (ASPA).

References

Paul, R., & Elder, L. (2009). *The miniature guide to critical thinking: Concepts and tools* (6th ed.). Dillion Beach, CA: Foundation for Critical Thinking Press.

Shafritz, J., Russel, E., & Borick, C. (2011). *Introducing public administration* (7th ed.).New York: Pearson Education, Inc.

Cohen, S., Eimicke, W., & Heikkila, T. (2008). *The effective public manager: Achieving success in a changing government* (4th ed.). San Francisco, CA: Jossey-Bass (Wiley).

Holcombe, R. (2006). *Public sector economics: The role of government in the American economy.* Upper Saddle River, NJ: Pearson Education.

All About Fear: Retrieved December 06, 2012, from http://www.psychologytoday.com/basics/fear.

Barack Obama. (n.d). BrainQuote.com. Retrieved December 20, 2012, from BrainQuote.com website; http://www.

brainquote.com/quotes.

Michael Griffin. NASA. Retrieved December 20, 2012, from http://www.nasa.gov/about/highlights/griffin_bio.html

The Universal Declaration of Human Rights. Retrieved December 28, 2012 from http://www.un.org/en/documents/udhr/index.shtml#a7.

Dikembe Mutombo Foundation. Retrieved December 30, 2012, from http://dmf.org/index.php.

Buchholtz, A., Archie B. (2009). *Business & Society: Ethics & Stakeholder Management.* (7th ed.) South Western.

Merriam-Webster Online. Retrieved January 2, 2013, from http://www.merriam-webster.com/dictionary/coordination.

Merriam-Webster Online. Retrieved January 2, 2013, from http://www.merriam-webster.com/dictionary/Cooperation.

Merriam-Webster Online. Retrieved January 2, 2013, from http://www.merriam-webster.com/dictionary/collaboration.

William Shakespeare. (n.d.). BrainyQuote.com. Retrieved January 3, 2013, from BrainyQuote.com Web site: http://www.brainyquote.com/quotes/quotes/w/williamsha101484.html.

Abraham Lincoln. (n.d.). BrainyQuote.com. Retrieved January 3, 2013, from BrainyQuote.com Web site: http://www.brainyquote.com/quotes/quotes/a/abrahamlin109274.html.

Bruce Lee. (n.d.). BrainyQuote.com. Retrieved January 4, 2013, from BrainyQuote.com Web site: http://www.brainyquote.com/quotes/quotes/b/brucelee394186.html.

The Library of Congress: Retrieved January 3, 2013, from http://www.loc.gov/wiseguide/oct05/revolution.html.

The Structure of the Government Must Furnish the Proper Checks and Balances Between the Different Departments: Retrieved January 4, 2013, from http://www.constitution.org/fed/federa51.htm.

O'Sullivan, E., Rassel, G. R., & Berner, M. (2008). *Research methods for public administrators* (5th ed.). New York: Pearson/Longham.

Cooper, T. (2006). *The Responsible Administrator.* San Francisco: John Wiley & Sons.

Vince Lombardi. (n.d.). BrainyQuote.com. Retrieved January 13, 2013, from BrainyQuote.com Web site: http://www.brainyquote.com/quotes/quotes/v/vincelomba127517.html.

Justice as a Virtue. Retrieved January 13, 2013, from http://plato.stanford.edu/entries/justice-virtue/.

Selective Mutism. Retrieved January 15, 2013, from http://www.social-anxiety.com/area-selective-mutism.html?gclid=CLnSnPjH67QCFQ_hQgodg0AALg.

Chronicle. Retrieved January 17, 2013, from http://www.chron.com/news/article/Data-show-Nigerians-the-most-educated-in-the-U-S-1600808.php.

Academic of American Colleges and Universities. Retrieved

January 18, 2013, from http://www.aacu.org/about/statements/academic_freedom.cfm.

H. L. Mencken. (n.d.). BrainyQuote.com. Retrieved January 21, 2013, from BrainyQuote.com

Web site: http://www.brainyquote.com/quotes/quotes/h/hlmencke157559.html. http://bible.cc/proverbs/14-1.htm.

Yahoo Contributor Network. Retrieved February 10, 2013, from http://finance.yahoo.com/news/first-person-had-no-savings-40-retired-60-180400536--finance.html.

Amy Poehler. (n.d.). BrainyQuote.com. Retrieved February 14, 2013, from BrainyQuote.com Web site: http://www.brainyquote.com/quotes/quotes/a/amypoehler436978.html

Cash for Clunkers. Retrieved February 15, 2013, from http://www.cashforclunkers.org/.

The Casualties. Retrieved February 15, 2013, from http://expertscolumn.com/content/poetry-analysis-john-pepper-clarks-casualities.

John Donne. (n.d.). BrainyQuote.com. Retrieved March 13, 2013, from BrainyQuote.com Website: http://www.brainyquote.com/quotes/quotes/j/johndonne101197.html.